MOUNTAIN BIKING THE COLORADO TRAIL

MOUNTAIN BIKING THE COLORADO TRAIL

TIPS, TRICKS, AND WHAT YOU NEED TO KNOW FOR A GREAT BIKEPACKING EXPERIENCE

MICHAEL J. HENRY

trails books
AN IMPRINT OF BOWER HOUSE
DENVER

www.BowerHouseBooks.com

Photos by the author
Designed by Margaret McCullough
Maps by Rebecca Finkel

Printed in Canada

Library of Congress Control Number: 2023933950

Paperback ISBN: 978-1-934553-81-7
Ebook ISBN: 978-1-934553-84-8

10 9 8 7 6 5 4 3 2 1

Disclaimer: Risk is always a factor in backcountry and bicycle travel. Many of the activities described in this book can be dangerous, especially when weather is adverse or unpredictable, and when unforeseen events or conditions create a hazardous situation. The author has done his best to provide the reader with accurate information about backcountry travel as of the writing of this book, as well as to point out some of its potential hazards. It is the responsibility of the users of this guide to learn the necessary skills for safe travel, and to exercise caution in potentially hazardous areas, especially on steep and difficult terrain. The author and publisher disclaim any liability for injury or other damage caused by backcountry traveling, or performing any other activity described in this book.

For
Andrea, Em, and Jo
and Ed Itell

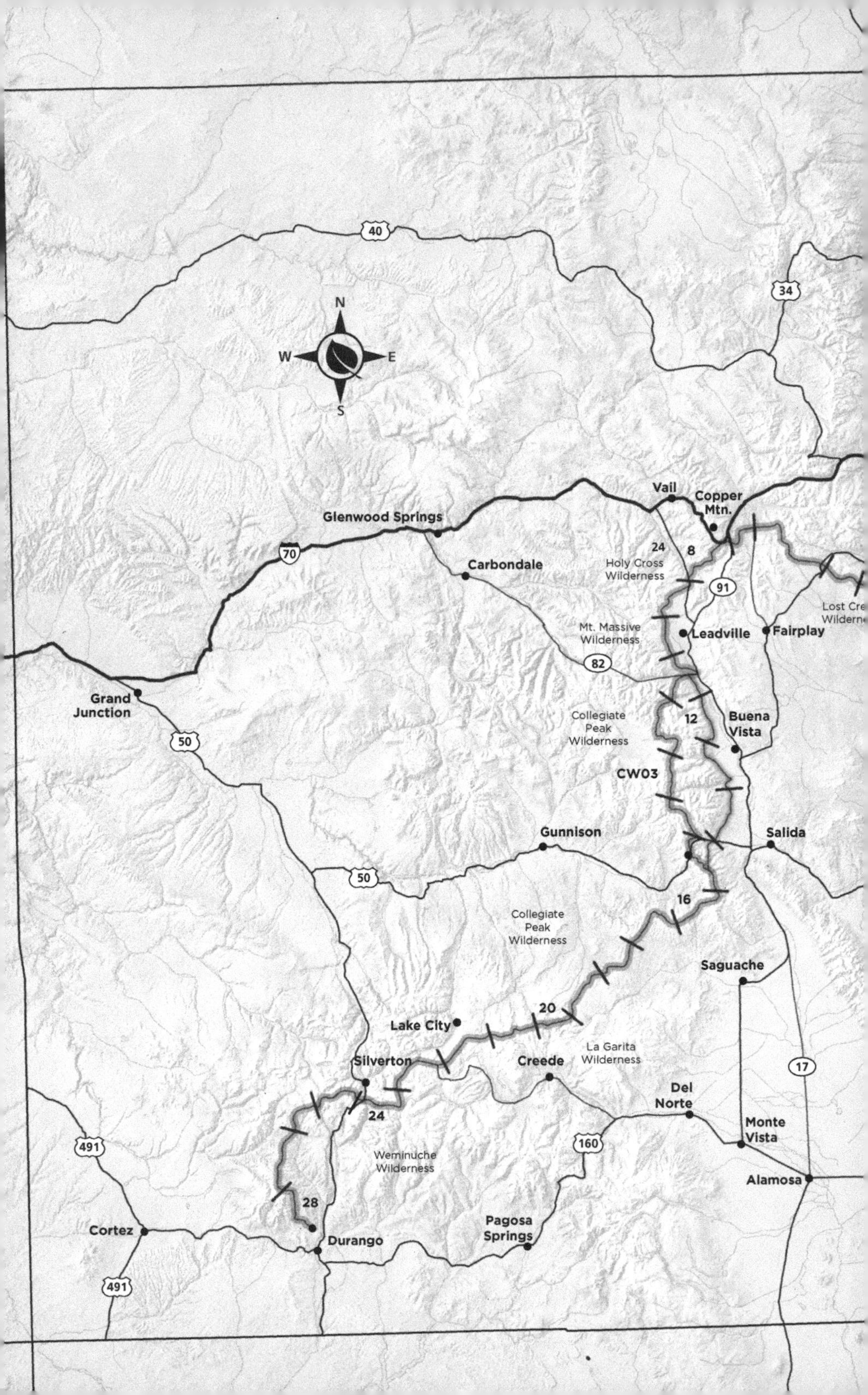

40
34
N
W
E
S
Vail
Copper
Mtn.
Glenwood Springs
70
24
8
Carbondale
Holy Cross
Wilderness
91
Lost Cre
Wildern
Mt. Massive
Wilderness
Leadville
Fairplay
82
Grand
Junction
Collegiate
Peak
Wilderness
12
Buena
Vista
50
CW03
Gunnison
Salida
50
16
Collegiate
Peak
Wilderness
Saguache
20
Lake City
La Garita
Wilderness
Silverton
Creede
17
Del
Norte
24
Monte
Vista
491
160
Weminuche
Wilderness
Alamosa
28
Cortez
Pagosa
Springs
Durango
491

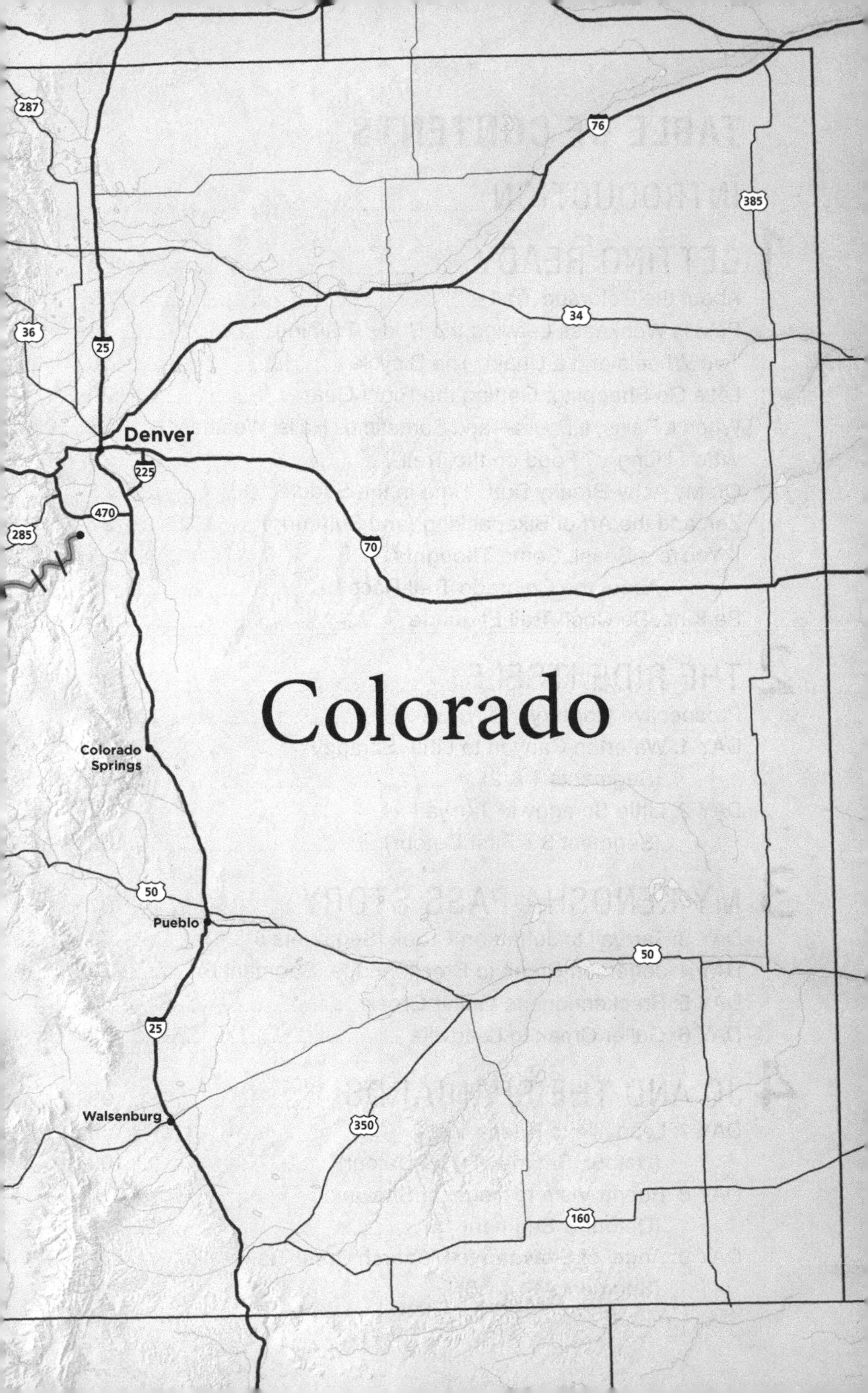
Colorado
Denver
Colorado Springs
Pueblo
Walsenburg
287
76
385
34
36
25
225
470
285
70
50
50
25
350
160

TABLE OF CONTENTS

Uncertain as I was as I pushed forward, I felt right in my pushing, as if the effort itself meant something. That perhaps being amidst the undesecrated beauty of the wilderness meant I too could be undesecrated, regardless of the regrettable things I'd done to others or myself or the regrettable things that had been done to me. Of all the things I'd been skeptical about, I didn't feel skeptical about this: the wilderness had a clarity that included me.

—Cheryl Strayed, *Wild*

Walk away quietly in any direction and taste the freedom of the mountaineer. Camp out among the grasses and gentians of glacial meadows, in craggy garden nooks full of nature's darlings. Climb the mountains and get their good tidings. Nature's peace will flow into you as sunshine flows into trees. The winds will blow their own freshness into you and the storms their energy, while cares will drop off like autumn leaves. As age comes on, one source of enjoyment after another is closed, but nature's sources never fail.

—John Muir

Beauty was not simply something to behold; it was something one could do.

—Toni Morrison

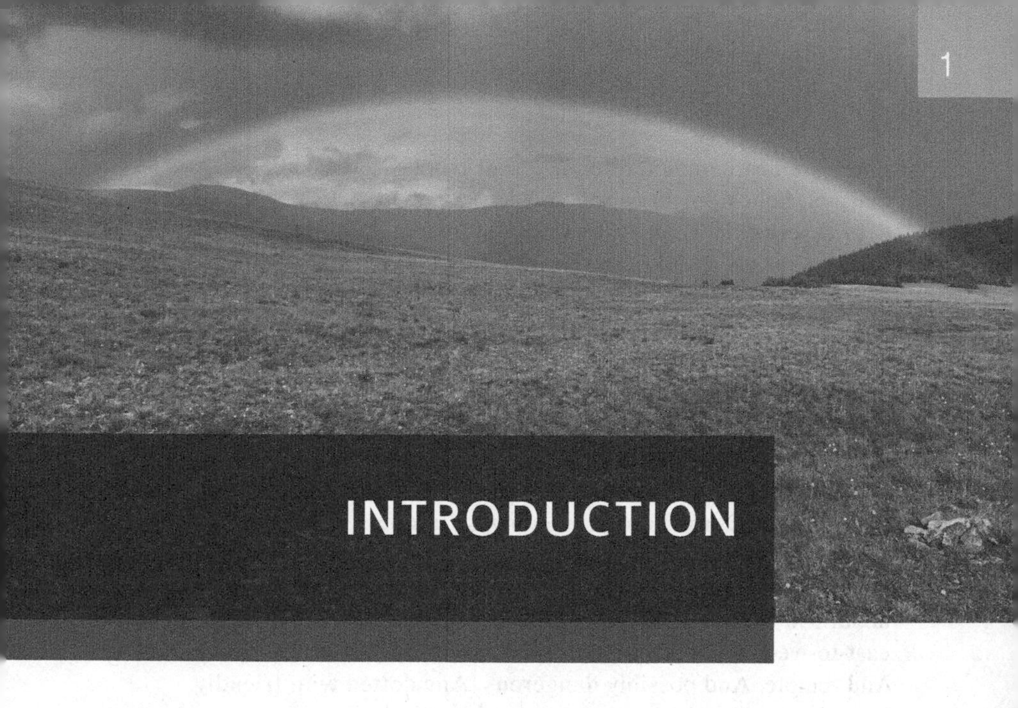

INTRODUCTION

My first day riding the Colorado Trail, I reached an outlook somewhere in the middle of Segment 2 and stopped to take a break, sheltered by a tower of boulders. I was tired and overheated. I climbed off my bike and sat in some shade. Completely alone, the only sounds were birdcalls and a gentle breeze in the pines. Strange for Colorado, the air was humid; the grand, hazy vista of rocky outcroppings and evergreen forests resembled an impressionist painting.

The beauty and solitude held my breath for a moment and I felt, for the first time in a very long time, both my humanity and my smallness, one infinitesimal being in the midst of all this nature. I didn't know what might happen on this journey—who knows what waits beyond the next bend in the trail?—but I knew that while it might not be easy, it would be memorable, an experience that would transform me.

As I lingered in this epiphany, I heard a rumble of thunder in the distance, as if the trail gods were telling me to stop lazing around and get back on the bike.

The vista I'd reached was true and typical Colorado, which is a place like no other, with incredible panoramas of earth, sky, and forest, marked by rugged, remote mountain ranges, fields of gold and green, snow at any time of the year, and sunsets that leave one in awe at their sublime beauty. Vertically, the Centennial State stretches from 3,315 feet above sea level up to its highest point, Mount Elbert, at 14,433 feet.

LEFT View from Segment 23.
ABOVE Mountains in the haze of Segment 6, Georgia Pass.

There are bears, mountain lions, prairie dogs, rattlesnakes, eagles, marmot, bobcat, bighorn sheep, elk, pika, moose. Its people, too, defy description, running and riding hundreds of miles at a clip, eating all sorts of wild food (Rocky Mountain oysters, for example) and drinking all sorts of libations, most notably craft beer. Not to mention marijuana—from 2014 to 2020, sales blazed close to nine billion dollars.

Yes, this is the Mile High state, one that might seem to tower over all the others. I say this not to belittle others—I'm originally from New York—but it provides a bit of context when thinking about traversing the state on a ribbon of mostly dirt, from Littleton in the east to Durango in the southwest: a route known simply as the Colorado Trail.

The Colorado Trail, the CT as I'll sometimes call it, is long—about 530 miles by bike. It is hard—over 70,000 feet of climbing, east-to-west, the most popular direction. And yes, it is gorgeous. And remote. And possibly dangerous. And dotted with friendly, historic towns and other cool stops along the way.

The Colorado Trail is all these things, and more. It's a physical route, of course, but it's also an experience. One in which you will challenge yourself, exploring your deepest fears and grandest hopes. If you ride it, you'll learn about your literal and metaphorical heart. You'll also learn and relearn practical things, like how to set up a tent, in the dark, during a rainstorm with gale-force winds, when you are utterly spent. Or, how to repair things—a tire, a shoe, a shifter cable, a chain—with duct tape, wire, torn clothing, or tools you've never had to use before. Or what contact dermatitis on your butt feels like. (Unless you have a mirror handy or are very flexible, you won't learn what it looks like.) Or how heavy a bicycle can feel when lugging it up the face of a mountain, and how to sleep in deep cold, even in the middle of summer, curled up in a sleeping bag in the actual middle of nowhere.

Riding the Colorado Trail, you'll learn things about physics and weather, about your mind, body—and heart. And I promise: you'll never forget your time on the CT. It becomes part of you. You'll find yourself recalling details years later, often at the most unexpected moments.

If you ride the entire CT, over the course of a few days or several summers, you will end up a new person, and the effort will very likely confirm what you already knew about yourself: you are a badass.

RIGHT Top of Georgia Pass.

THE WHY OF IT

I've told so many people this, my wife can only roll her eyes when she hears it again for like the 47,000th time: In my senior year high school yearbook, the quote I chose to go with my portrait was one I'd found in a massive *Webster's* dictionary my mother kept in the living room alongside some *Reader's Digest* condensed novels. It was from the Greek philosopher Seneca, and went like this: "A man struggling against adversity is a spectacle for the gods."

I know how to endure—if there's one thing I'm good at, one talent I possess, it's this fact. I've always been a slow and sometimes reluctant starter, but once I get going, I find my pace and I'm on my way. I find myself renewed and recharged by the work—by the struggle against adversity. And yes, there is something noble, maybe even transcendent, in such an endeavor.

As a teenager I tried many sports—basketball, hockey, baseball—but lacked the coordination and aggressiveness necessary for success. Luckily I found distance running, for which I possessed some natural ability, and so distance running it was. A skinny, sensitive, head-in-the-clouds kid, the solitude and self-punishment of track and cross country fit my personality as well as my body. When I reached my early 30s, I traded my running shoes for a mountain bike, and now I find myself suffering—in a good way—surrounded by the wonder of the natural world, chasing thin lines of dirt toward a pure, often fleeting, sense of bliss.

It's taken some time, but I've come to realize that the physical lessons of distance running and mountain biking helped me deal with other life challenges—namely my parents' divorce and my mother's too-young passing from lung cancer. Both events were long and drawn out, and at many points I wanted to quit, but had to keep going. What other choice is there? One must keep moving forward. You can't run away from it, and you can't bury it, because eventually it will claw its way back to the surface and demand your attention. Therefore, you must endure the pain, the heartache. Maybe even learn to embrace it, and use the wisdom gained for the next challenge, whatever it may be.

Perhaps those attracted to long-distance sojourns like the Colorado Trail are like me: drawn to long stretches of difficulty, physical and otherwise. We love solitude and the sense of renewal it provides. We love being places where few others have been, wrestling with fear and self-doubt. We want to see how far our bodies and spirits can take us. From such journeys we gain confidence, perspective, wisdom. We forge a deeper connection with the natural world and with the inescapable passage of time. For what is life but a long, sometimes exhausting, yet magnificent, journey?

Mountain biking the Colorado Trail, then, is a microcosm of life. There are moments of great challenge and pure joy. It can be expensive, in both time and money. You alienate yourself from loved ones as you focus time and energy elsewhere. The journey begins and you quickly encounter many obstacles, many tall mountains to climb. You get lost and must look back in order to gain perspective and find the way forward. You end up hungry and exhausted. You crash, dramatically—or stupidly. (You're standing at a trail junction, taking a quick break. Suddenly you lose balance and fall over, for no reason—that sort of thing.) You find grace and kindness in surprising places. You get your dumb ass saved by total strangers, and this gives you hope for this insane, dumpster-fire of a world. You become reacquainted with your true self. And you pause sometimes, to fully take in the unspeakable beauty all around. You escape the trappings and pressures of modern existence and reacquaint yourself with the basics, somehow cleansing yourself of all the weight of your life. You learn, or relearn, what's important and what is frivolous.

On the Colorado Trail, all this living is compressed into a handful of days. Whatever your reason, you'll have time to mull everything over. You'll question your sanity and intelligence. There will be time for extended conversations with yourself, or your riding partners, to figure out solutions to problems you never had time to consider before. Memories will well up from the depths, and you'll savor them. Some you'll want to forget, but they'll stay with you as you pedal, and walk. You might be serving as a spectacle for a god—or several—but in my experience, they usually aren't vocal about it. And yet, sometimes, often at the very moment you need it, you'll feel the hand of some invisible force guiding you, pushing you on. A rainbow might suddenly appear in a storm, a vision at the exact moment you most need it, or the trail will smooth out and you'll roll along, almost weightless, right when you feel like giving up. I know it sounds strange, but such moments of grace do happen, and maybe that's one of the reasons why people ride the Colorado Trail. It's certainly worth it.

And that's really my advice, if I have any. Keep your mind and heart open to everything that happens, good or bad. This life you're leading is the one you're supposed to be leading. The trail you're riding is the one you are supposed to be on.

HOW TO USE THIS BOOK

This book is a how-to guide for bikepacking the Colorado Trail. It includes all the important information a mountain biker needs to know,

ABOVE Getting Close to Durango Sign.

and also tells a little bit of the story of my experience on the CT, which I rode solo over the course of three summers. This book is not meant to serve as an exhaustive data or directional source; the *Colorado Trail Guidebook* and *Databook* published by Colorado Trail Foundation are the comprehensive resources for directions, maps, mileage, campsites, water sources, and geologic details. As good as those books are, however, they don't include much bike-specific information. After all, the Colorado Trail is primarily a hiking trail—something you'll learn very quickly once you get out there. Here I attempt to serve as an integral experiential resource for riders, complemented by the *Guidebook* and *Databook*. I also hope that the stories and information contained within are not only helpful, but maybe even a tiny bit entertaining. Adventures like this are only helped by one's ability to find humor in the difficult, the absurd, the surreal, and the breathtaking.

ABOVE Gold Hill.

COLORADO
TRAIL

1 GETTING READY

ABOUT THE COLORADO TRAIL

The biking route for the Colorado Trail runs about 535 miles. It crosses eight mountain ranges and detours around five wilderness areas. Average elevation is around 10,000 feet above sea level, which means that, compared to sea level, there's about 30 percent less oxygen for your lungs to take in. The trail's lowest point is at Waterton Canyon, the eastern terminus, 5,511 feet above sea level. The highest point reaches an altitude of 13,271 feet, just below Coney Summit on Segment 23.

Numbers seem to vary, but if you ride from east to west, the most common direction, you'll climb more than 72,000 feet. That's a whole lotta up, so gird your loins.

About 300 miles of the CT are single- or double-track. The rest are dirt or paved roads—mostly occurring on wilderness detours, which run through resupply towns such as Leadville, Buena Vista, and Silverton. You'll also swing by Breckenridge and Copper Mountain on your sojourn, so you can be smart—or lazy—about how much grub you want to carry, and if you're like me, you might want to procure a motel bed for one—or more— blissful nights of sleep along the way.

Is this cheating, you might ask?

Hell no, that's not cheating. You have my full permission.

LEFT General Colorado trail blaze.
ABOVE Above the Gudy Gaskell Bridge, marking the beginning of Segment 2.

PAIN IS WEAKNESS LEAVING THE BODY: TRAINING

The old-school philosophy on training for something like riding the CT is simple: just ride ride ride your ass off for at least four—or six, or twelve—months. This can be a combination of road cycling and mountain biking, obviously with a preference for the latter.

If you're looking for a training plan that's a little more structured, I have some suggestions, based on what I've learned in my 40 years as an endurance athlete, lots of self-directed research, and conversations with other experts, most notably Scott Gurst, founder and head coach of the Brute Squad, training group associated the Boulder Mountain Bike Alliance. There are, of course, myriad possible resources. You could hire a coach. You could join a team. You could become a Strava afficionado and devise your own training regimen based on the app's suggestions and online resources.

Basically, riding—and, to be honest, hiking—the Colorado Trail is a long, slow, aerobic endeavor. If you're pushing yourself above aerobic threshold too often, you're probably going too hard. If you're racing the damn thing, then you probably know a lot more than I do about training, so never mind.

In general, it's best to break your training into three phases—something I learned a long time ago as a collegiate distance runner at University of Rochester. *Go Yellowjackets!*

PHASE 1: BUILDING THE BASE

Otherwise known as long, slow distance (LSD) training, here's where you start out. Your goal here is to build an aerobic foundation while getting the body used to ever-increasing mileage. Most of these rides will be well below aerobic threshold—the point where you're sucking wind so hard you can barely keep up—and should be an effort you could sustain for a few hours without too much trouble. A simple guide: you should be able to carry on a conversation during these training sessions.

This is where you train your body to be more efficient at processing oxygen, where you get your muscles used to long efforts. You won't be over-taxing your body here, since the goal is to gradually make it ready for quantity, not quality, of effort. While the focus is on steady effort below excessive strain, on a bike—especially a mountain bike, which is all about climbing mountains—this doesn't mean you won't be exerting yourself. On long climbs, especially. The trick will be to find a balance between quality of effort and time of effort. Finding those prolonged, gradual climbs and going up, up, up in a way that is sustainable for long periods of time. Again, this is about quantity, not quality.

For those with heart rate monitors and such, these workouts are focused on Zone 2, which is less than 70% of your max heart rate. For me, Zone 2 is around 120 beats per minute, as my maximum heart rate tops out at about 170 beats per minute. Does that sound too easy? Well, yes, it does. But that's how it works. Just remember: these workouts should be long—at least an hour. And as you build up, total time should increase—to two, three, or more hours.

WHAT THE HECK IS LACTATE/AEROBIC THRESHOLD?

Good question! Let's see if I can summarize: Lactate or aerobic threshold is the level of effort where your body cannot take in enough oxygen for your muscles to work while burning fat, and begins to switch to the less-sustainable burning of sugar and carbohydrates. Recent studies suggest that this process is a gradual one, not an absolute on/off switch. However, once you make the switch—and when this happens an athlete is sucking serious air—lactic acid begins to build up in muscle tissue, and that eventually limits one's ability to keep up the level of effort, because the muscle can't work as efficiently. It also hurts, like, a lot.

The idea is to increase the body's ability to process oxygen—to raise one's lactate threshold, in other words—so you can sustain longer and longer periods of hard effort. If you can process more oxygen more efficiently, the body can do more work at a faster pace without burning out.

In terms of numbers, lactate threshold (LT) is about 85 to 90% of your maximum heart rate, measured in beats per minute. Maximum heart rate can be simply estimated by subtracting your age from 220, but varies with genetics, training history, and athletic ability. I'm 55 years old, so: 220 – 55 = 165. But I've been doing this for a long time, and as I said above, I've noticed that my maximum hovers closer to 170. So for me 90% of max heart rate = 145 to 153. My experience bears this out: once my heart rate gets to about 150, it's clear that I'm working hard. My respiration changes, my focus changes, my body changes. Things get real, in other words. I know I can stay there for a while, but not forever.

PHASE 2 : SPEED AND STRENGTH

Once you've built a good, strong base, then you can begin to build strength and lactate threshold training into the mix. Your mileage might decrease a bit here, and you should remain in this phase for a good part of your training. My opinion is that a 50/50 split between LSD and speed and strength is a good measure to aim for.

This block of training will involve getting right up to lactate threshold (LT), teasing it, and going above it periodically for measured periods of time. The extent of time should vary—from 30-second pedal-mashers, usually uphill, that are unsustainable for much longer, to one-minute pushes, two-minute pushes, and longer sessions of work around "race pace," right at LT. You may do a series of these intervals—four, six, ten—but break them up with recovery periods. Do these sorts of intense workouts once, maybe twice, per week, and never on consecutive days. The harder and shorter the push, the longer the recovery. For example, to borrow from my running life, every Wednesday during University of Rochester cross country season, Coach Hale would get us on the track, doing 12 to 16 intervals of one lap—400 meters—a little faster than race pace, usually around 70 to 74 seconds each, with 90 seconds of recovery in between. Occasionally, he'd alternate recovery time, with every other break shortening to 60 seconds.

This kind of speedwork also helps prepare the body for going fast—getting your legs acclimated to pushing hard, generating serious power. The more often you do that, the longer you'll be able to sustain such an effort, and the faster your body will recover. This work will also get you used to hard pushes when you're out on the trail. It'll also build your confidence and mental toughness. On the bike, these sessions could focus on climbing or pedaling hard in a big gear—that's where the effort gets real. You'll get better at climbing and generating power, and you'll also get stronger.

In these kinds of workouts, as your body gets taxed, you'll begin to get tired earlier and earlier in each interval. After time, when you're really becoming a beast, you'll notice a change. You'll get further and further into the repeats before tiredness hits. That's when you really know you're getting into good shape. These workouts are also good at helping you measure effort—in other words, how to pace yourself and dose out effort so you don't totally bonk.

To complement interval workouts, which should happen at least once per week, your other hard workout should be a sustained effort. An extended ride close to threshold, kind of like one, long interval, is good. This shouldn't last too long—an hour seems like a lot—but the longer you go, the easier your pace should be. The idea is to sustain the effort for the entire duration, not to crush yourself, but to get *close* to bonking, if you know what I mean. Preface all these hard-effort rides with an earnest warm-up and follow them with a cool-down, to keep the blood flowing and to help your muscles flush out any lactic acid. Also, try not to go out too hard and end up slowing down. Sustainability is key here—you want to choose a pace that's hard, but one you can maintain through the whole workout.

Training at and sometimes above threshold is the most important work in this active phase 2, but it's not the only thing. In between, you'll want to continue modest LSD rides. Go long—but not stupid long—and go easy enough so you can have a conversation with a riding partner and not get too out of breath. Once a week, go long and slow. As you build through this phase, your long rides should approach your ideal daily mileage for the CT, and then some. Forty, fifty, sixty miles, easy, with little climbing, is what you're shooting for.

During this period, it's also important to eat right, get enough sleep, and to take care of yourself. Be sure to stretch. You're breaking your body down in order to build it up stronger, so you need to replenish it daily. If you don't, you'll either get injured or sick, and then you'll be forced to shut the training down until your body can get back to normal.

TO GIVE YOU A CLEAR IDEA OF WHAT I'M TALKING ABOUT, HERE'S A SAMPLE WEEK OF WORKOUTS IN PHASE TWO:

MONDAY: *Intervals.* 8 x three-minute climbs, hard, each one followed by two minutes rest. You should be suffering mightily, and sucking serious wind at the end of each. Twenty-to-thirty minutes for warm-up and cool down. Heart rate should approach maximum during the later stages of these efforts, and you should not be able to chat with anyone, especially at the end of each interval.

TUESDAY: *Easy one-hour ride.* Stretch.

WEDNESDAY: *45-minute to 1-hour steady state ride.* Think long climb, or road-ride at a good pace. Conversation is possible, but you should only be able to squeeze out short, simple sentences. Heart rate should be about 70% toward maximum, or a little bit under aerobic threshold. You should be breathing hard, but not out of breath, and you should be able to sustain a given pace for the duration. Bracket this with at least a 10- or 20-minute warm-up and cool-down.

THURSDAY: *OFF!* Try some strength training or yoga. Or an easy townie ride.

FRIDAY: *Easy maintenance ride.* Like Tuesday's pedal.

SATURDAY: *Go be a real mountain biker.* Don't think about training. Do some serious climbs, some serious downhills, have some fun with friends. Drink beer. And/or a milkshake.

SUNDAY: *Long, slow ride.* This should be your highest mileage effort of the week.

PHASE 3 : PEAK MAINTENANCE

Often called "tapering," during this phase you gradually ease up and rest your body before the big effort. A week or two before embarking on your ride, ease back on the hard workouts and the mileage a little bit, and move back to a slower pace. Easing up allows your body to recover and prepare for the Colorado Trail. In this phase, you're merely maintaining peak fitness. Don't stop riding completely; you still have to get on the bike and do some work.

STRENGTH TRAINING

This, too, is important, Grasshopper. Strengthening the upper body, core, and legs is very useful when you're slogging 65 pounds of bike and gear up a steep, mile-long boulder field at 11,000 feet. I'd recommend a fair amount of strength training during Phase 1, and then maintenance during Phase 2. Too much during Phase 2, with all the hard riding, might cause problems.

Think squats, leg extensions, upper-body exercises for the chest, shoulders, back, triceps, and core exercises, especially sit-ups and back work. Dynamic work—lunges, jumps, and other explosive repetitions, are good, too. And again: don't forget stretching—you'll want to keep those muscles lean and flexible—especially your quads, iliotibial bands, calves, hamstring, and piriformis.

Perhaps you're wondering: Mike, did you seriously train like this? Well, here is where I proclaim the proverbial teacher's mantra: do as I say, not as I do. Or did.

My training was not terribly focused or well-planned, but over the course of three summers I was able to modify based on what I'd learned. And what I learned helped me clarify one deep truth: your training should get you used to riding many hours a day, day after day. Proper training makes a huge difference. Your ability to power the bike in July or August will very much depend on work done in March and April.

I tried to ride about 1,000 miles in the months leading up to my trips, mostly a combination of road rides and mountain biking. I attempted to climb at least 3,000 feet vertical on every mountain bike ride, seeing as an average day on the CT would require more than that. To prepare for my last jaunt, I did lots of intervals, lots of long rides, and lots of strength training, and the difference was immediately clear. I was faster, I rode longer, I suffered less, and pretty much enjoyed everything a little more. During training, I did not ride with a fully-loaded bike, something I perhaps should have done, something I encourage you to do at least a couple of times. It'll make your first day on the CT a little less of a shock, and you'll build power while getting used to how a fully-loaded bike handles, whether it's grunting up a climb, railing a downhill, or walking.

Training lazy like I did is perhaps the bare minimum for the work you should put in. It *might* prepare you for long days at high altitude, but you won't go fast, and you will probably suffer more than you need to. (Trust me.) And if you think you don't have to train and can ride yourself into shape, well… I will light a candle and say a prayer for you.

So, in general, how much should you train in terms of overall mileage, et cetera? Good question.

I'd say your baseline—your minimum—would be what I did for training in 2019. In the six months before I hit the CT from Molas to Durango, I rode 1,090 miles, an average of 181 miles per month.

Man, as I type this I'm thinking: that is paltry and sad.

On the other end of the spectrum, CT rider Ben Handrich (see my interview with him later in the book) said he rode about 200 miles per week. For several months.

In summary: don't be like Mike, be like Ben. Or at least be somewhere in between.

ABOVE Marshall Pass aspens.

INTERVIEW WITH SCOTT GURST

Head training coach of Brute Squad,
workout group of Boulder Mountain Bike Alliance

Q. *First, tell me about Brute Squad.*
A. Brute Squad stands for BMA Riders United in Training for Endurance, and BMA is the Boulder Mountainbike Alliance. We're a training group that focuses on a 16-week program to get riders ready for a race that we choose every year—usually something over 50 miles in length. We work together as a group, but each rider receives a customized training program. Coaches give feedback throughout the training period, and we work hard, but it's really about building community and camaraderie. We start training in April and go through the summer, culminating in the race. During that time, we host fun events along with training sessions.

Q. *How many riders participate?*
A. About 30 to 40 every year, starting around 2013.

Q. *How'd you get into coaching?*
A. Growing up, my parents ran a summer camp, so I've been leading people in activities for some time now. I started coaching runners, and then when I gradually moved to mountain biking, I started coaching mountain bikers.

Q. *What general advice do you have for someone training to bikepack the CT?*
A. Specificity is important. By this I mean that you should prepare for the specific actions and work you'll be doing on the trail. The body adapts to what you train it to do, so you'll want to simulate, as best as you can, what you'll be doing every day as you travel from Waterton Canyon to Durango. Singular distance over the course of one day isn't the challenge with the Colorado Trail—it's the work you'll be putting in multiple days in a row. That's what your body needs to get ready for. Give your body that experience before you hit the trail by riding long days, doing a fair amount of climbing over the course of several days in a row. If you can, do this with your bike fully loaded. Not only will your body get prepared, your mind will

be familiar with how it feels, and what the challenges might be. This extends out to other things, too, like hydration and food. During your training, practice eating and drinking as you'll be doing it on the CT. And yes, be on your bike in beautiful places; try to make it enjoyable and fun, too. It shouldn't always be a painful slog.

Q. *How far in advance should a rider begin to train?*
A. That depends on a lot of factors, but not too soon. Sixteen weeks is a good framework.

Q. *What's a good structure for training?*
A. Three days a week of hard work is enough. For Brute Squad, we train hard on Tuesdays, Thursdays, and Saturdays. These are shorter, high-intensity efforts, working to improve lactate threshold and increase VO2 max. Some efforts also focus on building power—short bursts of hard effort, usually uphill, often over challenging terrain. The key is to vary these types of hard efforts. Keep them interesting.

For example, one might focus on going above lactate threshold, where you're totally out of breath at regular intervals. Another might be a "sweet spot" workout where you extend an effort just below threshold—about 90 to 95% of max heart rate for a longer period of time. Something like four pushes for eight minutes each, with two minutes recovery is good. Or hill workouts where you pedal hard, uphill, for two 20-minute sessions, with a solid break in between.

Then, up the intensity and shorten the duration: do a series of uphill 30-second bursts, or 16 pedal revolutions, in a huge gear, absolutely as hard as you can, with a short break in-between—thirty seconds is good. This really helps build power.

On your easy days, go easy. Get some low-intensity miles in, where your heart rate is in Zone 2, which is around 70% of maximum heart rate. It'll seem so easy; you'll be able to chat with fellow riders. This level of training not only increases aerobic capacity, it burns fat, too.

One more detail: make sure to take every fourth week easy. Let your body recover and adapt.

Q. *What other sorts of training would you recommend?*
A. Don't just ride. Develop your overall fitness—in addition to power, endurance, leg strength, work on upper body and core

strength. I'd suggest lifting weights and cross training as well. And test all your gear out. Experiment with food and hydration beforehand, too. Once you start, you don't want any surprises.

TWO WHEELS AND A CHAIN: THE BICYCLE

"The bicycle is the most civilized conveyance known to man. Other forms of transport grow daily more nightmarish. Only the bicycle remains pure in heart."

—Iris Murdoch

As with most elements of preparation for the CT, you'll have several important binary choices to make. Such as: hardtail or full squish? Fat bike or regular tires? Dropper or rigid post?

One's bike is as unique as one's signature, so these are very personal choices. Some firmly believe there's no need for full squish and all that extra complication is just more stuff that can break. Others can't live without a rear shock. Then there are those special humans who are suspicious of multiple gears and derailleurs in general and forgo them for a single-speed adventure. For many of us there's not much choice: you'll ride the bike that's currently in your garage. That's okay, too.

My garage is home to a full-suspension Specialized Stumpjumper FSR 29er with a dropper post. I was very happy to ride this bike on the CT. Did I maybe end up pushing it a mile or two more than I would have if I had a slightly lighter hardtail? Maybe. But I love my bike. I'm used to how it rides, and I deeply appreciated the dropper post—except for those few times when it mashed my Revelate seatbag into the spinning rear wheel (but only because the bag wasn't snugly secured). Downhills went smoothly. At Kokomo Pass, for example, two Spanish thru-riders rode up on their hardtails and hit the downhill about ten minutes before I did. I quickly caught and screamed past them. So I guess if I'm going to give you any advice, it's this: ride the bike you have, love, and feel most comfortable on.

Whatever kind of steed you saddle up, make sure that everything is tuned, prepped, and ready to go. Your tires should be relatively new, with enough sealant if you're tubeless—which I highly recommend, by the way. (I've been riding tubeless for about 15 years. During my whole CT ride, I never once had a tire issue.) Even if you are riding tubeless, bring at least one tube, just in case. Make sure your chain is newish and well lubed. Bring a few extra links, and a chain-breaking tool. Check that your brakes are in good working order; bring a spare set of pads, and know how to replace them. If you have a handlebar bag, make sure it's set up properly and isn't crushing your cables—especially if you have a dropper-post cable. I crushed my cable two days away from Silverton and almost had to ride the rest of the way with my seat at its lowest point. Not good. Luckily, I'd brought some electrical tape and jimmied up a solution. (Handlebar harnesses work well for this sort of thing.) If you're riding clip-ins, check that your cleats are tight, and bring an extra set in the off chance that one gets mangled or you lose a bolt. And if you have a front and/or rear shock, set the air pressure to take into account the extra weight you'll be carrying—about 25 to 35 pounds in most cases.

Finally, here's some obvious advice, which you've already heard, and will hear again: test out your ride, fully loaded. You don't have to suffer up a ten-mile climb, but some up and down would helpful. That way you'll have a sense of how the bike is going to handle—both riding and walking. This is especially true if you have a bunch of new upgrades: try them out before you hit the dirt. Tweak as necessary. Get rid of stuff that doesn't work, or drives you nuts. Tighten things that get loose. Be familiar with how it all works, and how it packs up. The latter will save you time each morning when you break camp and are freezing your tuckus off. Also, know at least some basics of bike

ABOVE Bike loaded up.

repair. Figuring out how to fix something when you're on the CT in the middle of nowhere is not much fun, and there probably won't be an easy connection to YouTube so you won't be able to learn on the fly. And honestly, just the stress of worrying about possible unsolvable mechanical problems can mentally wear you down.

LET'S GO SHOPPING: GETTING THE RIGHT GEAR

Ah yes, gear. The accoutrements that get bolted, strapped, taped, bungeed, hung, and welded to the bike or placed on your person, objects that will keep you (relatively) comfortable. And alive.

Like your bicycle, your choices will probably be a pastiche of what you already currently own, what works for you, and what you find at the latest sale at REI. And that's okay—as long as you like it, as long as it works, as long as you can afford it. You absolutely must try everything out, even if it's to snuggle in a sleeping bag for an hour while watching YouTube videos of Danny MacAskill on your cell phone. Familiarity makes for good friends.

CLOTHING

Clothes aren't exactly heavy, but they can take up a lot of space, so you don't want to carry too much. I know this from personal experience: When you end up bringing something you don't end up using, each day that item gets physically heavier and heavier. It's weird but true. And yes, weight is an important factor in your general happiness.

In general, you'll want three sets of clothing, some of which may overlap:

DAYTIME RIDING OUTFIT: Comfortable short-sleeve shirt; riding shorts with chamois; a solid pair of socks; riding gloves. I prefer full-finger gloves, but others might choose to go with less. If you're not a huge fan of sunscreen, a buff and lightweight sleeves are good alternatives.

APRÈS-RIDING AND SLEEPWEAR: Comfortable shirt (long-sleeve is a good idea); casual shorts or long pants (long-johns or sweats); comfy socks. A face covering or buff if your nose gets cold in the night. A pair of camp-shoes are good here, but they can be bulky to carry over the course of 500 miles. (I brought a pair of Teva sandals on my trip, strapped onto the outside of my seat bag.)

LOUSY-WEATHER GEAR: Long pants or leggings; a rain-jacket; long-sleeve shirt or arm sleeves (can repurpose long-sleeve sleeping shirt here); extra pair of heavier socks (wool is good, can also double as sleeping-and-camp socks); warmer gloves if your hands are delicate; a hat/head-covering, like a balaclava or skull cap, that fits under your helmet. It can get viciously cold out there on the trail. The jacket and pants should be waterproof.

HELMET: Get a good one that's comfortable.

SUNGLASSES: A must-have. For those of you who live in Colorado, you already know this. If you're coming from, say, the East Coast, you may be a little taken aback by the quantity and strength of sunlight here in the Centennial State. Also: be sure to bring, or have available, a cleaning cloth. Sweat dripping on lenses will be a problem.

SHOES: Again, a binary conundrum—cleats or flats? You could go either way here. They both have pluses and minuses. Flats are way more comfortable, and since you'll be hiking quite a bit, they'll make your life easier. But cleats allow for a more efficient pedal stroke and better control. My recommendation is to split the difference and wear cleated shoes that are more like hiking shoes—with comfort in mind, as well as traction.

As for me, I wore my usual cleated shoes. I feel much better when I'm clipped in and have been riding in them since I first got on a mountain bike. They were more like XC shoes, and therefore kind of sucked—okay, totally sucked—on long hike-a-bikes. I slipped a lot, my feet ached terribly, and so on. Next time I get back out on the Colorado Trail, I will definitely be wearing shoes that allow for more comfortable and stable hiking.

HOUSING/SHELTER

This is one I obsessed over. I actually lost sleep—in my pillow-topped king-size bed, before I embarked on my sojourn—by obsessively considering all the options, over and over. I did hours of research, studying a hundred different sleeping philosophies—bivy, hammock, quilt, bag, big tent, small tent, tarp, emergency sleeve, nothing at all, and so on. I have a good friend who swears by a hammock sleep system, so I bought all the gear for it, but chickened out after trying the full kit in the backyard one fine evening—hammock and straps, bug net, over-tarp, sleeping bag, etc. It just didn't feel right, and I'm glad I bailed. I would have had a helluva time finding the right spot, the right trees to tie onto, and so forth. Plus, I don't know how to tie knots—I can tie my shoes but that's the most complicated tying I can handle.

I ended up using my 30-year-old Clip Flashlight two-person tent. It packs up super-small, it's light, and ridiculously easy to set up. Some riders will go with even less—an over-tarp and a sleeping bag and that's it. But I'm not like that, and in the end decided that the single pound of extra weight was worth it. And I was glad of my choices when it rained, hard, all night, a couple of nights. But if you're good at tying knots and dealing with tarps and bivy sacks, or really feel cozy sleeping in a down jacket on hard ground, give it a go.

BEDDING

I don't know about you, but I'm generally a happy, positive kind of guy. And yet there is one thing that can put me in a murderous, nihilistic, bad mood: lack of sleep.

As I may have said before, I'm not exactly a youngster. I am perhaps old enough that escapades like bikepacking through the Colorado high country are a little dumb. I am not a terribly fast rider. I like a real bed. I use a CPAP machine for sleep apnea. I'm also a side sleeper, but have this weird issue with my ears—I can't handle too much pillow-pressure on my ear; it gets hot and aches and puts me in a rage. I can't sleep unless the pillow is shaped just right, with a little, hollow indentation for said ear.

All of which is to say: I am worse than Goldilocks.

I pretty much have my system dialed in—good tent, extra warm bag (did I mention that I'm also a really cold sleeper?), decent pad, hat, face covering, pillow with a notch for my soft, tender ear. It took a long time to get to this point where I feel reasonably comfortable.

Still, though, I tended to sleep poorly on the CT.

I guess such is the suffering I'm destined for, being such a delicate flower. I very much hope you are not so delicate and can enjoy a blissful evening of sleep and tender dreams no matter where you are, that your home situation is something akin to a bed of nails. That way, your entire Colorado Trail experience will be in general better than most. For sleep is the sweet elixir of life and will give you the mental sharpness, the guts, and the ambition you'll need while out there. A good night's sleep gives you wings.

Okay, now that I've stated the obvious—sleep is important!—let's talk about set-up.

As I've said a thousand times already, test your kit before hitting the dirt. This will most likely be a perennial strategy-and-data-seeking mission. You'll constantly be working to improve your sleeping situation, as well you should. It can always get a little better.

In general, you'll want:

A STURDY, COMFORTABLE SLEEPING PAD. Something that handles your body and preferred sleeping position—back, side—without compressing too much and exposing you to the unforgiving hardness of the earth underneath. Since I'm a bony-hipped side sleeper, a good sleeping pad is a prime necessity. Besides cushiness, one that's easy to pack is imperative, and one that you can blow up without getting too dizzy and lightheaded is good, too.

A PATCH KIT. It sucks massively when you have to roll over multiple times each night, in the middle of the night, and blow up your pad after it's been leaking for a few hours. I got a slow leak on my trip and spent three really lousy nights having to slide off the pad and reinflate it several times each night. That was not enjoyable. If I'd had a patch kit, I could have solved the problem in about ten minutes. You may need to locate a water source—ideally a stream or pond—to submerge the thing in order to find the leaky spot.

A SLEEPING BAG THAT WILL KEEP YOU WARM WHEN THE TEMPS GO BELOW 30 DEGREES. Which is not to say get a 30-degree rated bag. I'm a super-cold sleeper, and wake up cold even when it's 35 degrees out and I'm in a 20-degree bag. In general, it can get pretty close to freezing on the Colorado trail in July and August, so be ready. If you're a warm sleeper, you can skimp a little. It's always better to err on the side of warmth, though.

Over the course of my three-year ride, I bought three different sleeping bags. One was too big—it literally didn't fit in my handlebar bag. The other was very nice, but I froze my ass off, even though it was rated to 30 degrees. I ended up spending a good wad of cash on a tall (I'm 6' 1") 20-degree bag from REI. In all my time on the trail, I don't believe temps went below 35 degrees, but it made a huge difference.

SLEEPING CLOTHES THAT YOU LOVE. I won't even try to go into the time-worn *Do you sleep naked or do you sleep clothed in your sleeping bag?* discussion. You know what you prefer. Personally, I'm a fan of warm bottoms and top, and super-warm socks. Wool is good. Fleece, too.

A NIGHT CAP (CAN ALSO BE YOUR RIDING SKULL-CAP) OR BALACLAVA if your schnozz gets cold easily. I am bald and shave my head, and I have a big nose, too, so I'm all in with the balaclava.

A PILLOW YOU'D BE ABLE TO SLEEP ON AT HOME. I went through a host of potentials before settling on a very small inflatable version that didn't have any ear-related annoying pressure points, as mentioned earlier.

A TENT THAT'S EASY TO EXTRICATE ONESELF FROM in the middle of the night when one wakes and has to pee like a proverbial racehorse. Most tents accomplish this pretty well, even my ancient Clip Flashlight, which I bought back in 1992. It must pack up small, and it must handle rain well. Otherwise, you will be miserable, because at some point, you will get rained on.

Every person's shelter and sleep system is a personal choice. Find what works for you, tweak as necessary, practice setting it all up and tearing it down, and then pack it all up and hit the dirt.

Sweet dreams, riders.

KITCHEN

Simply put, carrying a stove is a kind of a pain, but a necessary one if you don't want to go with cold food the whole time. Weight and packing space costs are not insignificant, but it's all about the experience you want to have. There's something pleasingly meditative about cooking your own food in the wilds after spending a long day on the bike. The warmth in your belly is nice, too. Same with making a hot cup of coffee in the morning as the sun warms the world.

There are lots of stoves out there that burn isobutane or propane, or a combo of the two. Common brands are Whisperlite and PocketRocket. One fuel canister should get you through if you're only cooking breakfast and dinner, but if you have room, a back-up can't hurt. Or, when you get to Buena Vista, which is just about the half-way point, grab a new canister and toss the old one. Bring something that makes flame, too, so you can make a campfire if there isn't a ban in place, and to light your stove if the damn auto-lighter apparatus stops working, like mine did. A regular old Bic lighter will do the trick.

TECH

I could devote an entire book to just this topic and it still wouldn't cover all the options. I'll try to keep it short and direct by outlining what I think are essentials, and then go from there.

Essentials include your cell phone and any charging cords you might need when you get back to civilization and can plug in for some free juice. A battery backup charger will be integral, because there are a few sections where you'll be in the wilds for a few days and will need a recharge—just be aware of weight and bulk. One way to conserve battery power is to put your phone in airplane mode when you don't need to be tied to the grid. The phone's GPS will still work, but won't be forever roaming for a cell tower or Wi-Fi connection. And yes, you'll want your phone. It's a very handy emergency device (if there's cell coverage), it's a great way-finder (see below), and most phones nowadays are pretty good at taking pictures and video, too.

In general, your phone can handle all that, plus there are several apps that'll show where you are in real time—the best of which is the FarOut (formerly Guthooks) CT Trail app. Make sure to purchase the mountain biking version, which has all the directions for the wilderness detours. It's absolutely amazing—clear maps, exacting (and therefore sometimes depressing) elevation data, timely notes from other trail users on water sources, trail issues, and more. If you're a super careful person, or if you have a nervous partner or parent who needs to know where you are at all times, someone who freaks out as soon as you leave their sight, you could bring along additional protection in the form of a personal locator beacon or satellite phone.

Other trail tech: there are myriad choices—Strava for tracking your effort, for example, but also additional locator apps like AllTrails and MTB Project. They're all good. I especially like the MTB Project Colorado Trail app—it has some good data on the CT. Like FarOut, it provides exacting detail on where you are, and I suppose it's nice to have a little redundancy.

PERSONAL CARE

To keep yourself fresh, protected, clean, and pretty, here's what you'll need:

SUNSCREEN AND LIP BALM—both are essential.

TOOTHBRUSH AND TOOTHPASTE. Be a true pro by cutting down the handle of your toothbrush, saving at least 1/10th of an ounce. Otherwise, you're just an amateur.

CAMP TOILET PAPER AND BIODEGRADABLE WET WIPES, OBVIOUSLY. And if you're planning on digging post holes for burying your business, a small trowel.

A FIRST-AID KIT with bandages, butterflies, gauze, tape, antibacterial ointment. Just in case you need it. Most likely, you will.

CHAMOIS BUTTER. Sure, if it works for you. (It gives me a rash.)

DEODORANT. But really, why the heck for? I suppose if you don't enjoy the aroma of pure, unadulterated nature on your own body, then fine.

HAIRBRUSH OR COMB. (No hair, like me? No need.)

SOME CAMP SOAP AND A TINY CAMP TOWEL. A good idea, for sure—cleaning oneself makes curling up in a sleeping bag a much more relaxing endeavor. You will get filthy, and there will be many camps near water to bathe in.

NAIL CLIPPERS. Totally bring a pair.

ANY PRESCRIPTION MEDICATIONS, EYEGLASSES AND/OR CONTACTS.

VITAMIN I—IBUPROFEN—IS ESSENTIAL.

SOME PEPTO-BISMOL OR TUMS TABLETS, in case you get a sour tummy.

Honestly, that's about it. Remember: except for the stretch between Monarch Pass and Silverton, you're never more than a day or two from a town or supply station.

PACK BAGS

Now that you have all this stuff, you need something to put it in, something that'll keep it safe, dry, and snugly attached to your bike. There are myriad systems, but in general there are four types of bags: handlebar; frame; seat; cockpit. There are other places to store stuff—on the downtube and forks—mostly to hold water bottles. Seat bags are great, yet tend to shift and bounce a little when you're rolling down bouncy stuff—called "tail wag"; handlebar bags will shift too, but they have more points of contact and therefore tend to be a little sturdier. Frame bags are the best, but can't always hold a ton. Be sure to get one that fits your bike frame, and be aware that a full frame pack will most likely not allow for an upward-facing bottle cage.

If you're riding a full suspension, finding a good frame bag will be more of a challenge; you might need to get one custom made. In general, a solid handlebar bag will store sleeping gear and tent; seat and frame bags can hold clothing, food, and tech; cockpit bags are good for daily food and snacks, and maybe your phone—or other tech you need handy—and the little CT trail book. If you're thinking about panniers, make sure you can handle the unpredictability of a mountain bike trail before taking off. In general, panniers are better for bike touring, not mountain bikepacking.

As for cost, be ready to drop some pretty serious cash, though there are often lots of decent used goods out there. Just make sure the Velcro is tight and the zippers work well. You don't want one busting open while on the trail.

In terms of brands, I'm a big fan of Revelate. There's also Apidura, Ortleib, Oveja Negra, and Blackburn. Some riders like to make their own, too.

For more information, a great resource is bikepacking.com. They have great reviews and advice on all things bikepacking.

BOOKS

Well, of course, bring this book with you! (You really can't survive without it.) But for exhaustive directions and specific info, the *Colorado Trail Databook* is an absolute must. Pocket-sized and weighing less than four ounces, it has all the numbers and directions you could ever want. You could bring the *Colorado Trail Guidebook*, too, but it's bigger and heaver. Both are published by the Colorado Trail Foundation.

You could also bring a favorite book of poetry, or Thoreau's *Walden*, or something similar. There might be some down time when you'll want some sage, poetic passages to mull over. If you're a total weight weenie, you could tear out pages after you've read them and burn them in your evening campfire.

WHEN IT RAINS, IT POURS— AND SOMETIMES HAILS: WEATHER

If there's a single element that ties all this talk about gear together, it's weather.

In the course of my Colorado Trail journeys, I got rained on, hailed on, and baked by the hot sun. I spent a harrowing hour at 12,000+ feet, huddled against a rock outcropping as lightning railed down all around me. I spent entire days under a cloudless sky with temperatures climbing to 90 degrees and above. At one point, on a detour, I huddled under a tree and my tent tarp in a frigid downpour. Eventually I gave up, riding up the road to a cheap motel where I promptly checked in, took a scalding hot shower, and climbed into bed—in the middle of the afternoon. I froze my ass off on more than a few nights, only to get cooked by the sun a few hours later. One morning, above treeline, I literally crawled for a stretch through a howling, hurricane-force wind.

ABOVE Raincoat on Georgia Pass

The next morning, I rode through a lovely, dewy dawn, freezing my ass off, yet wearing pretty much every article of clothing I had with me, including a pair of cold-weather gloves.

I did not get snowed on, but that would not have been unusual, even in July or August. (If you're traveling in June, the chances are a good deal higher—it regularly snows in Denver mid-May, and much later in the high country. Same for September, especially in the San Juans.) One good thing about Colorado weather—as wild as it can be, it generally doesn't rain non-stop for days on end, and in general humidity tends to be low, which means you and your gear will dry out pretty quickly if you do get soaked. In general.

All of which is to say: be ready for a wide variety of conditions. The Colorado high country can produce any kind of weather at any time, and you should be mentally and physically prepared to slog through some really lousy weather. You should also be prepared for day after day of calm, cloudless, big blue skies and oceans of stars each night.

If I had to suggest a best-weather time of year to ride the Colorado Trail, I'd easily go with early to mid-August. The days are still long, and it's usually past the typical afternoon thunderstorm pattern, known in Colorado as the monsoon season. Then again, each year writes its own weather story, so you never know.

Which reminds of an old saying—the only thing you can really do about the weather is complain.

WHO'S HUNGRY? FOOD ON THE TRAIL

If you like to break down complex projects into basic building blocks, the foundation upon which an endeavor is built, listen up. The four most important elements of riding the Colorado Trail are:

1. FOOD
2. WATER
3. BIKE/GEAR
4. A MONOMANIACAL, BRUTAL DEDICATION TO MOVING FORWARD

Obvious, right? And yet, such a statement reveals an infinite number of challenges to overcome and decisions to be made.

I'd like to talk a little about that first element—food—and what sorts of concerns one should apprise themselves of, and so forth.

When I rode the CT, each day contained more than a little fretting about food. What to eat? When to eat? Do I have enough? Will this upset my delicate tummy? Do I really want to stop *yet again* to scarf down calories?

And so on. It got a little crazy-making.

My advice to you is this: Try to bring more food than you think is enough—and eat it.

Don't over-ration if you don't need to. And you shouldn't need to, if you've planned well and hit resupply stops at the right time. Carrying tons of food is no fun; I know from experience. But it's better than walking your bike, weak-legged and dizzy, your vision occluded by low-blood sugar, at 11,000 feet with not a single fellow human in sight. At my slothful pace I averaged about 30 miles per day and consistently felt starved. I would try to avoid eating too much during morning and at lunch, and then by mid-day I'd be exhausted and weak.

As my Italian grandmother often implored, when I was a skinny little kid: *Eat! You're a good boy, but you don't eat.*

Obviously, I didn't always plan well—meaning I didn't carry enough food—and at one point near Sargents Mesa it was clear I was going to starve to death before getting to Leadville. Some poor hiker would eventually find my remains, my bone-and-gristle hands clutching my handlebars, my skull still encased in a Giro helmet. It was not a good feeling. *Alas, poor Yorick! Methinks he did not bring enough grub.*

Thankfully, amazingly, when I exited the singletrack of the Mesa I came upon a camp of trail angels. And angels they were, those lovely ladies, Jan and Pooh, who'd set up a shelter with a grill and more food than you could imagine. I scarfed down three hot dogs right then and there. And an apple, and a banana. And three cookies and a bag of chips. They totally saved my dumb ass.

Most estimates say you'll need to consume at least 4,000 calories per day while on the Colorado Trail, and that's probably on the low end. (Normal everyday numbers are 2,500 for men, 2,000 for women.) In my totally uneducated estimation, you need more like 5,000 calories per day.

At the very least, know thyself and how you need to eat when riding all day. Before you hit the CT, try some all-day rides with food to see how you how it goes. You might not be like me, you might have a hollow leg that naturally stores glycogen. Still, you're going to need food, and lots of it.

So, what to bring? High-calorie foods, but not all junk. Sure, eating eight candy bars a day would be awesome, but you also need real food. Gels and energy bars are helpful, but if you're like me, they won't quite fill you up and you'll burn through them quickly.

And while you can't bring along a side of ham, a loaf of bread, and a jar of mustard (I wish!), there are some things you can do.

BIG FOODS—LUNCH AND DINNER

CHEESE AND SUMMER SAUSAGE: Always good because they're filling, they're easy to handle, and require no cooking. Plus, they're packed with flavor, which is always nice when you're out there in the wild. Be sure to pack a hard cheese; they last longer without refrigeration.

PREMADE BURRITOS: Some bikers swear by them. They buy a bunch of frozen burritos or make their own, and go with as many as they can carry. And who doesn't love a burrito? They're calorie-rich, and filling. I'd shoot for a mix of rice, beans, cheese, and whatever else seems tasty. I'd probably skip the beef burrito, though (no refrigeration). If you go exclusively this route, you could forgo carrying a stove. You'd miss out on hot dinners and morning coffee, but you might save some weight—and packing space. But then you'll be eating cold burritos, which have their own disadvantages. Namely, getting them down the gullet. *But* then again, they are substantial. (Now you see the endless back-and-forth that can happen.)

FREEZE-DRIED FOOD: Many swear by those dinners-in-a-bag—mac-and-cheese, lasagna, potatoes, alfredo, and so on. And they're great—they weigh nothing, they pack down well, they get you fed. I've tried a bunch of different kinds and most are just okay. Except for Idahoan Four-Cheese or Buttery Homestyle potatoes—those are pretty freaking tasty! However, an entire package—four servings worth—can sometimes be a little hard to scarf down. I guess you need to take into account: it's not really about enjoying every bite, it's about replenishing energy stores. Personally, I really like regular supermarket-brand items. Idahoan of course, and Knorr is good, too, especially their alfredo and four-cheese risotto. For protein, mix in some salmon or tuna in a pack. Then you'll have something resembling an actual dinner.

Perhaps it's just my own taste, but the fancy freeze-dried dinners you buy at REI and other outdoorsy stores are pretty awful. My taste buds aren't yours, however, so try a bunch of different meals out before you hit the trail. Find what works for you, taste-wise *and* digestion-wise. The last thing you want while riding the CT is to feel not quite up to par digestively. That'll ruin your trip and might even force you off trail.

BREAKFAST ITEMS

If you're bringing a stove, instant oatmeal, oatmeal, and more oatmeal! There are also breakfast packs of freeze-dried eggs and various meats—like bacon and sausage. (Personally, I thought they were pretty gross.)

Instant Coffee. Single-serving tubes of coffee work very well. Bring a baggie with sugar and powdered milk mixed together—the must-have in my book. You could always bring the mini brew-drip apparatus for a daily fresh, hot brew. Remember, though, it's about choices, and once you begin loading up your bike, it quickly becomes apparent that you'll have to make some tough decisions about what stays home and what goes with you, what you absolutely need and what you can live without.

SNACKY SNACKS

JERKY: I love jerky! But if I eat too much it makes me feel sick, which is sad, because it's a staple item for many—the protein helps you feel full, it packs well, and it's calorie-rich. Try not to overdose on the stuff; most jerky has high sodium and cholesterol content.

ENERGY BARS: I'm a fan of the Clif Bar crunchy peanut butter and chocolate chunk with sea salt. RXBar Protein Bars are also tasty and packed with good stuff, like nine grams of protein.

SNICKERS BARS: A classic favorite out on the trail. Allegedly, research has shown that they have the right mix of simple and complex sugars for a quick burst *and* sustained energy, and the peanuts offer a bit of protein.

GELS: bring a gross of your favorite; you can't go wrong. Don't squeegee too many caffeinated packs into your gut; otherwise you might have a restless night's sleep—or should I say, an even more restless night's sleep, considering you'll be sacking out on the ground, in a tent or under a tarp, in the high-country cold.

PEANUT BUTTER: Single-use packages from Justin's are great; slather them on your energy bars or tortillas for an extra boost. (My wife, who grew up in Las Cruces, New Mexico, is scandalized by this thought—tortillas are for beans and cheese, nothing else.)

DRIED FRUIT / TRAIL MIX / GRANOLA: I've heard, and maybe you have, too, that real food is supposed to be good for you. Try to avoid the dried fruit or trail mix that's coated in a veneer of sugar. Trail mix with some M&Ms isn't too bad—as long as there's lots of other stuff in there, like nuts and raisins. But no coconut flakes. Yuck.

HYDRATION POWDER: I'll talk more about this below, but you absolutely need to bring something. I recommend whatever you usually drink when you ride. The CT is not the best time to try out something new.

WATER

As much as anything, making sure you have enough fresh, filtered water is crucial. You won't survive without it. There are myriad filtration systems out there, and I have to tell you that there is nothing more satisfying than drinking a deep draught of ice-cold mountain water that you've just filtered. It's amazing. It cools you off and immediately boosts your energy and happiness quotient.

In terms of what to carry it in, well, a CamelBak type of drinking system works well for bikers. I used a 3-liter Osprey pack that also held my rain gear. I also had a cage for a water bottle, which I'd fill with water and drop in some Skratch Labs powder, and that worked beautifully. Speaking of that, you will want some sort of hydration powder. You can be fully hydrated, but if you've lost too many electrolytes, you're screwed.

The CT *Guidebook* and the FarOut app will be your indispensable go-to resources for finding water on the trail. Occasionally, you might have to do some hunting, but there will almost always be clues of human activity: gently trod grasses by a tiny, tricking stream; small rock-dams set up to pool water and create a mini-waterfall for you to fill up your water bottles/jugs/bladders/Nalgenes/SmartWaters. I love coming across someone's handiwork—a carefully positioned large green leaf that creates a sluice, carrying the water into something resembling the silver arc of a drinking fountain. It's like a little forest fairy made it just for a thirsty fool like me.

A couple of deeper thoughts: It's fine to bring a pre-filter to avoid drinking the murk you sometimes end up with, but if you choose not to, you'll be okay. In general, water sources on the Colorado Trail tend to be fairly clear. And if you do end up drinking some little bits of organic material, which may or may not include mosquito larvae, and which may or may not be very nourishing, in my very un-medical opinion you'll be fine, you'll be fine. For my part, I did not bring a pre-filter and never really stressed about it.

Try not to contaminate any part of your filtered water—a drop or two from outside your cleaning container can theoretically mix in and re-contaminate everything. Third, be wary of mosquitoes when you're collecting water. It's a necessary annoyance, but it's good to be aware—or to have some repellent handy—when you're ready to gather some H2O. Otherwise, you could be standing there, collecting your hydration from a slow trickle, as your precious blood is slowly stolen by a thousand mosquitoes. Very annoying. And itchy.

ABOVE Waterfall past Kokomo Pass.

There are a multitude of filtration systems, including pump, gravity, ultraviolet (UV) wand (my choice), squeeze, straw, and chemical. Whatever you choose, be sure to either have a back-up—filters, batteries, or other needed elements—in case your system breaks down. Iodine tablets are a good last resource because they're tiny and effective. The drawback is they make water taste pretty lousy. A few Google searches will provide all the information you'll ever need, but in general REI is a trustworthy resource, whether it's online or in-person.

Whatever you do, don't drink untreated water. The likelihood you'll get sick is high, and there's really no need to take such a risk.

OH MY ACHY-BREAKY BUTT: TIME IN THE SADDLE

Riding, to put it simply, is a pain in the ass.

But not all pain is the same. Saddle sores, to use the common term, have many manifestations. They can surface as, well, a surface issue—when the skin on your bum gets tender, inflamed, ragged, irritated, bumpy, broken—all sorts of raw. The pain can seep deep as well, into muscles and bones—where you feel like you're bruising and/or breaking your glutes and sit bones. I've never heard of someone actually fracturing a sit bone while sitting on a bike saddle, but I wouldn't be surprised if it has happened.

And yes, sit bones are real things; the technical term is "ischial tuberosity." They're not technically bones themselves, but a part of one's pelvis. In all my extensive research (about 20 minutes of Google searching) I've found that pain in the sit bones is most often caused by poor saddle fit, but sometimes it's caused by the hamstrings and the ischial bursa, a small sac of fluid that has something to do with reducing friction between moving body parts, like joints.

Anatomy lesson aside, one of the obvious keys is to have the right equipment for your equipment. A good saddle that fits you well—you'll know a good fit after you've rested your behind on it for about couple of hours—and decent shorts with a good chamois. You'll also want to have the saddle set up properly. In general, this means the nose of the saddle is not pointed up or down—the whole thing should be parallel to planet earth. It should also be relatively neutral front or back, meaning that you shouldn't be reaching for your handlebars, nor should you be smashing your knees against your shift levers, either. Common consensus says that when you're pedaling, at the crank's horizontal position—three o'clock and nine o'clock, in other words—your front-leg kneecap should be directly over the center of the front pedal. One other item about bike fit: when your leg is fully extended and you're sitting in the saddle, you should have a *slight* break in your knee. Some of this is personal preference: I like my knee almost completely straight, while others like a little more bend. You'll find your own sweet spot by listening to your knees and hips; if things are not aligned well for your particular bod, you'll know, because it'll hurt, and not in a good way.

Another way to prevent the sometimes incredible, miserable pain a rider often feels in their nether regions on trips like this: ride a ton. In all truth, time spent in the saddle is really the only way to prevent saddle pain and soreness. The more you ride, the tougher your underhide becomes. That said, if you don't spend, say, a few weekends embarking on multiple-hour rides, when you hit the CT—and spend eight—or 10, or 16—days in a row in the saddle, you are going to get sore. Painfully sore.

In my experience, there are some treatments for this. Ibuprofen is one. The other is chamois cream, liberally applied, though in my experience chamois cream is a no-go. I'm somehow the lucky person whose bum seems to be powerfully allergic. When I use it, I get contact dermatitis—in other words, a wicked rash.

Washing out your chamois and shorts every evening is an important strategy that allays any rashes, soreness, and gross factor. You can use camping soap, and if possible, let the chamois see the light of day while drying. Sunlight helps it dry faster obviously, but also kills mold and mildew (ew!), the kind that gives off that musty smell.

Speaking of shorts, what about a great pair of riding shorts, with a super-supple chamois? Sure, that goes without saying. You will want a comfortable, sturdy, well-fitting pair of shorts or bike tights. Size will be important here, for when the shorts and chamois are soaked through and you've lost maybe a pound or two. And be sure that the actual stretchiness of the chamois, or tights, if you're that sort of rider, is still vibrant. An old pair whose compression abilities are shot will only cause you to be droopy and sad.

ZEN AND THE ART OF BIKEPACKING (AND SUFFERING)

"I've come to realize that mind is no other than mountains and rivers and the great wide earth, the sun and the moon and stars."

—Dogen Zenji

Now that we've covered many of the basics—training, bike, food, water, shelter, your buttocks—I want to talk a little bit about your brain and your soul, and how you might prepare them for riding the Colorado Trail. Sure, training the body and purchasing the right gear

ABOVE Rainbow on Georgia Pass.

are super important, but if your head isn't in the game, if you don't have the mental resilience and inner calm to deal with the exhaustion and stress, you're going to be unhappy and maybe even traumatized, and you might bail.

I have some advice, a combination of make-it-up-as-I-go-along philosophy and sensitive-ponytail-poet-boy psychology, but perhaps some it will resonate. As I've said before, I'm old, which means I am sage and gray, and I am also a poet, which means I have many profound and enlightened thoughts about this sort of thing.

I'VE BROKEN THIS MEDITATION INTO FOUR PARTS:

1. **Losing oneself**
2. **Ride your ride**
3. **Moving forward**
4. **Self-transformation**

ABOVE Approaching Engineer Pass.

1. LOSING ONESELF

Zen is not some kind of excitement,
but concentration on our usual everyday routine.

—Shunryu Suzuki

The resistance to the unpleasant situation
is the root of suffering.

—Ram Dass

The practice of Zen is forgetting the self
in the act of uniting with something.

—Koun Yamada

You may be wondering: what is the relationship between suffering and Zen practice? Well, if you've ever tried Zazen, which is basically nothing more than sitting with your legs criss-cross-apple-sauce and being mindful of your breath, after about 15 minutes the musculoskeletal agony caused by being thusly pretzeled up—in your neck, back, hips, knees, ankles, and more—will provide a fairly solid answer to that question.

Zen isn't only an exercise in pain, of course. It's the deliberate practice of "just sitting" or, more actively, just doing something simple over and over to the point where you lose sense of who you are, where you are, and what it is your body is up to. You are one with the action and one with the world around you; you are no longer necessarily conscious of the effort itself. For our purposes, instead of "just sit," it's "just ride."

While "just riding" the Colorado Trail, you may get lost in a million thoughts not related to the bike, the dirt below your wheels, or the effort. This isn't exactly Zen, I suppose, but it's getting there. As you continue on, you may gradually lose the distinction between self and the world around you, and you may find that your body is seemingly acting on its own. Now you're slipping into a Zen-like state. Along with just riding, and losing sense of the work involved, it's good to focus on your breath, the simple, renewing act of inhale, exhale.

Breath facilitates the trance-like state of mind of no-mind, where the body does what it does and decisions are made without internal deliberation or self-consciousness. Plus, breathing deep and even is just plain good for you.

Eventually, when you fall into Zen mindfulness you won't be thinking about how much pain you're in, or how tired you are, or how crummy the trail is. When your body is working on autopilot, that's best. Repetitive activity—like pedaling, like breathing—makes the process of losing oneself much easier. If you've ridden a lot, you know what I mean. It's a kind of wonderful, blissful fugue state, even though you're working your ass off.

There will be moments on the Colorado Trail where work, sweat, stress, and obsessive thinking will fall away and you'll course along in a dream-like, silent state. You'll be one with your body, the trail, the mountains and sky. You will be suffering, or at least exerting yourself, but you won't be focusing on the pain and difficulty. Instead of having your mind controlled by and reacting to the moment, your mind is *in* the moment. I believe that when this happens it's due to some alchemical combination of hard work over an extended period of time, embracing panoramic beauty, and probably some endorphins, also maybe some sugar (in the form of a candy bar or soda). It's also brought on by a letting go of all that you want and need. All the wants that drive you batty. *I want, I want, I want.* You want to be happy, you want to be safe, you want to be going faster, you want to feel strong and unstoppable, you want your saddle sores to go away, you want the rain to stop, you want the big rocks in the trail to not be there, you want a large pepperoni-and-banana-peppers pizza. (Letting go of that last one is really hard for me, personally.)

So many wants. Let them go. Breathe them away, pedal them gone. Accept *what is* for *what it is.*

Once you're out there, I promise you, it will happen: at certain moments the ride will become a Zen-like experience of total well-being, maybe even bliss. It won't make the effort any easier, honestly—but it will change the way you feel about it.

2. RIDE YOUR RIDE

What it comes down to is making the most
of what you are where you are.

—Thomas Hornsby Ferril

Start where you are. Use what you have.
Do what you can.

—Arthur Ashe

Riding the entire CT is not an easy endeavor by any means, and you might feel more of a sense of relief than victory when you finish. Any illusions you may have about your strength, stamina, intelligence, and sanity will be cast aside and your true self will be laid bare.

Are you ready for that?

Hell yes you are! You are a Golden God, I just know it.

If I may, a word of advice: don't worry about anyone else, don't even worry about your own expectations. Do what you can in the moment.

Go at your own speed. Don't worry if other riders, or even hikers, for that matter, pass you. Walk that bit of trail if you want to, and don't berate yourself because part of you thinks you should be able to clean

ABOVE Post Molas Pass, trail into the sky.

it. Skip a detour or two if you're not in the mood for a roadie slog. Sleep in a motel room if there's one available and the idea of it is comforting. In other words, be kind to yourself. Make sure to stop and literally smell the flowers once in a while. Look around once in a while, or very often. Again, you're going to go places where few people have ever been, landscapes of unspeakable wildness and beauty. Don't grunt your way through because you set a stupid goal for yourself. I say this to you even if you're racing. Know what your limits are, and feel okay about them.

This includes your gear and your prep. The bike you have is the bike you got. Sure, maybe you should have bought that $10,000 carbon ripper (what's a second mortgage good for, if not this?); maybe you should have ridden 10,000 miles in preparation. But as most parents—and grandparents, and coaches, and guidance counselors, and therapists, and sage grizzled old guys sitting at the bar—will tell you: *shoulda, woulda, coulda* ain't going to get you over the next mountain.

3. MOVING FORWARD

Life is like riding a bicycle. To keep your balance,
you must keep moving.

—Albert Einstein

If you can't fly, then run, if you can't run, then walk, if you can't walk, then crawl, but whatever you do you have to keep moving forward.

—Martin Luther King Jr.

I wake to sleep and take my waking slow.
I feel my fate in what I cannot fear.
I learn by going where I have to go.

—Theodore Roethke

When I was on my ride, I went so effing slow. Or at least it felt that way. Sure, there were moments when I cruised, but overall, when I checked my data, I'd average about 4 miles per hour—on a good day. Some days it was more like 2 miles per hour, mostly walking beside my bike.

Such is the experience of bikepacking the Colorado Trail.

As slow as I went, something miraculous happened: eventually, I finished the damn thing.

The lesson here is an obvious one: if you're moving forward, you're getting somewhere. Closer to the next camping spot, closer to the next town, the next brewery and pizza place, closer to the finish line. Would you like to eat up the miles like Payson McElveen? Sure. Will you, in all truth? Maybe, but most likely not. And that's okay.

Always keep in mind: nothing lasts forever. As slow as you might slog along, eventually you will finish the climb, the hike-a-bike, the boring dirt road. Eventually you'll cross over a ridge or pass, or enter/exit the woods, and a new landscape will greet you; most likely it will be as gorgeous as the last one.

If you're checking your progress on FarOut, Strava, or other app every three minutes, you'll end up driving yourself bonkers. I know this from personal experience. Endlessly checking progress makes the ride (er, hike) more brutal, annoying, and deflating. You never seem to get anywhere. This also relates to the Zen idea: if you're thinking too much about how slow you are going, if you're constantly checking to see how far you've gotten, you're in your headspace and aren't seeking "mind of no mind," which is much more fun.

For another take on this Zen idea, here's what author—and, I imagine, non-mountain biker—Walter Isaacson has to say:

> If you just sit and observe, you will see how restless your mind is. If you try to calm it, it only makes it worse, but over time it does calm, and when it does, there's room to hear more subtle things—that's when your intuition starts to blossom and you start to see things more clearly and be in the present more. Your mind just slows down, and you see a tremendous expanse in the moment. You see so much more than you could see before. It's a discipline; you have to practice it.

4. SELF-TRANSFORMATION

Our greatest weakness lies in giving up. The most certain way to succeed is always to try just one more time.

—Thomas Edison

Ever since I was young and discovered running, I've had a deep affection for suffering. I know that sounds odd, but suffering over long stretches of effort was really the only thing I was good at. As a freshman I tried out for JV basketball but didn't make the cut. Turns out you need to be able to dribble a basketball to make the team. That seems like some very fussy criteria to me, but whatever. Also, as a sensitive, skinny little kid, I swam in my emotions way more than other boys, and therefore I was eventually labeled—and considered myself to be—a total wuss, a wimp, a loser, a quitter. Eventually, when I finally realized that I really wasn't going to change this about myself, I was forced to consider: what if I embraced this part of my personality and built from it? What if I took my natural talent for suffering and sensitivity as a given? What if I learned to deal with suffering better than others, and learned never to give up? Would that not be a way to make my mark in the world, to show others—and myself—that I was good at something, that I had a talent I could dedicate myself to? Would not my sensitivity make me feel more alive, more appreciative and cognizant, of experience, whatever it might be?

My sensitivity surely played a role in my becoming a writer—specifically, a poet. I do think poets in general feel more deeply, and think more deeply, about the bittersweet paradoxes of everyday life—the passage of time, and yes, loss. Loss, which creates suffering.

I'm fairly sure I haven't suffered more than most people, and yet I have experienced loss in a way that allows me to endlessly confirm a lesson I learn every time I'm out there on the bike: pain, whether it be physical or emotional, is temporary. There's no use in trying to avoid it, so you might as well hold onto it and see what gifts pain might give you. Like wisdom. Or the confidence to deal with the most searing ache—physical or mental. Losing my mother when I was 24 certainly threatened to undermine my life, and yet, because I'd been running for so long, I knew to endure the weight of it. It didn't necessarily reduce the intensity of my grief, but it did allow me to be fully present in the moment, and to make of it what I could, because I'd done it before a thousand times before, in a much more modest, physical way. Because suffering and sadness happen and there is no way to make it not so.

Perhaps you're like me: you are familiar with pain and loss. You believe that being out on the Colorado Trail in full suffer mode will be somehow redemptive. You know the pain will cleanse you, remake you, give you perspective. You will learn again that nothing lasts forever, and that, if you keep going, eventually you will make it to higher ground. You will make it out of the wilderness with a new awareness of who you are and what matters, and with a new confidence. The popular term nowadays is *resilience*. That's a pretty good label. Learning resilience on the CT will help you be resilient in your own life, and yes, my friend, there will be losses and difficulty both on and off the trail (please see exhibit A: 2020 and 2021, the years that were), for what else is life, and the relentless flow of time, all about?

IF YOU'RE A BEAST: SOME THOUGHTS ABOUT THE COLORADO TRAIL RACE

Now if you're looking for the challenge of a lifetime and have legs like Earl Campbell, or if you once dusted Peter Sagan in a velodrome sprint, then perhaps the Colorado Trail Race is for you. In true Colorado style it's a fairly laid-back event using the honor system and some sort of tracking apparatus, which I tend to think of as a house-arrest ankle bracelet, though it's probably not like that at all. (Actually, it's a little fob that you carry with you.)

Every year, the race alternates direction, one year traveling southbound, the next, northbound. The general consensus is that northbound is more difficult, so you might want to take that into account. As of this writing, the fastest time recorded for the CT Trail race is 3 days, 19 hours, and 40 minutes, set in 2016 by Neil Beltchenko. The fastest woman's time is 3 days, 10 hours, and 15 minutes, set in 2022 by Lachlan Morton, riding north to south. More recently, Alexandera Houchin—riding a single-speed—completed the CT in 6 days, 1 hour, and 34 minutes. Just to give you a sense of the shenanigans that can occur. I mean, a single-speed? Good heavens. By all reports, only about half of the racers finish in a given year. In 2017, a particularly cold and rainy campaign, only 25% completed.

If a race isn't enough to get you going, or maybe you're not the competitive type but you're still looking for a challenge, you could always yo-yo: ride the entire trail, finish at Durango or Denver, take a deep breath, and then *turn around and go back*. At least that simplifies logistics: you don't have to worry about securing a ride back to your starting point.

Generally, and I am not speaking from experience here, since, again, I am not that ambitious, the race is lonely and arduous. There is no entry fee, no award, and no support. Most racers do not bring a tent or actual sleeping bag, and ride through the night, sleeping in fits and starts. Since it's a self-supported, individual time-trial, it's against the rules to seek out aid. In other words, you cannot ask for help with mechanical issues while on the trail, nor can you ask someone for food or H20. However, if someone offers, you can accept it. You can also ride into a supply town and get whatever you need.

For those seriously considering the race, my advice is perhaps not going to be very helpful. You are in a league above. I will say, though, that you should be familiar with these sorts of self-supported efforts, perhaps having tried a few shorter, less grueling ones to get prepped. And you should be riding your ass off—at least 200 miles per week—for an extended period of time. Your gear should be sturdy and well-tested in all conditions. You should be feeling in tip-top shape when you embark, for any little cough or sniffles will undoubtedly bloom into something worse. And you should be one of those people who can handle sleep deprivation. And, if you can, it would be good to pre-ride sections of the Trail, so you know what you're in for.

So, weather be damned, sleep be damned, comfort be damned! Just get on the damn bike and ride like the wind, young, incredible, wild-eyed person!

BE KIND, BE COOL: TRAIL ETIQUETTE

It's true: mountain bikers have a bad rap. Hikers, equestrians, and others think we're selfish, uncaring, crude, and rude when on the trail. Our job, dear CT bikepackers, is to undermine these assumptions.

How many times has this happened to you? You come up upon a pair of hikers walking down the trail, their backs to you. You're going slow because you are a kind, respectful human being/mountain biker. You are about to politely say *Howdy! Mind if I scoot by?* when they hear the crunch of your tires on the dirt. They startle, their bodies vibrating with sudden, immeasurable terror. They scream—in unison—and then they launch themselves into the bracken as if they've stepped on a land mine. They lie, broken and bloody, moaning and crying.

This has happened to me more times than I can count. And I firmly believe it happens because some other rider (or riders) have, at some point in the past, scared the living daylights out of these poor trekking-pole carrying folks. So the bad reputation must be deserved. I mean, who would act like that if they hadn't been traumatized before?

This all-too-common fear and loathing of mountain bikers comes from somewhere. And maybe you're like me: you're increasingly troubled and frustrated by some mountain bikers you encounter out on local trails. They don't slow down, let alone cede the right-of-way to uphill traffic. Or hikers. Or horses. Or whatever. They fly by at top speed, only sometimes getting out of the way, usually hopping off the singletrack to scarify the surrounding flora and fauna, widening the trail and eventually carving a double track where there was once only single. Some carry little speakers that crank out music you've never heard before—and which always, *always*, sucks.

Worst of all: when they pass by they don't even say hello.

This stupid jerk rider I'm describing is someone else, am I right? I mean, you and I? Never! We never do those things. And when bikepacking, we never do our alimentary business in the woods and leave it, unburied, for all to see. We never leave our campfires smoldering as we leave camp. We never ever leave wrappers and other garbage in the wilderness. We always pack out more than we carry in.

Right?

I don't need I say it, of course, because we are not like this, but I have to: Don't be that person.

Please, for the love of all that is spoke-based: stop for uphill riders, hikers, and horses. Be careful around blind corners—there's almost always someone just around the bend. Pack your garbage out. Don't pee near streams, creeks, lakes. When you go #2, bury it, and bury it deep.

And say hello to your fellow humans, maybe even give them a big, silly smile. You never know who they might be, what a conversation might illuminate, or how meeting someone out in the wilds just might soothe your soul.

SIERRA DESIGNS

2 THE RIDE ITSELF

I made it the mantra of those days; when I paused before yet another series of switchbacks or skidded down knee-jarring slopes, when patches of flesh peeled off my feet along with my socks, when I lay alone and lonely in my tent at night I asked, often out loud: Who is tougher than me? The answer was always the same, and even when I knew absolutely there was no way on this earth that it was true, I said it anyway: No one.

—*Cheryl Strayed,* Wild

The itinerary presented here roughly follows my own. The schedule is not only bearable, it allows time to enjoy the wilderness, to really immerse yourself in the indelible beauty and solitude of the Colorado Trail. It encompasses all the CT segments and biking detours, broken out into in a workable—and sane—17-day plan, though how far you go each day and where you eventually set up camp is a very personal decision, often made in a state of utter exhaustion and stupefaction.

Please note: riders more ambitious or in better shape could easily take less than 17 days. You don't have to camp where I camped, and you definitely don't have to go as slow as I did. Still, you can use this guide to combine days or patch together different segment combinations if you want to go faster. On average, it takes riders around 10 to 18 days to finish.

LEFT Camp Site After High Point
ABOVE Aspen leaves.

Each day's ride gets its own chapter, starting with a summary, including official CT segments, approximate total miles, and total vertical feet of climbing. I also include a few of my own measures of how fun, scary, hard, and scenic the day will be. I've devised a Suffer Quotient, which is not only scientific, it's mathematical.

Here are those gauges, defined. Each works on a scale of 1 to 5.

FUN FACTOR: Is the trail smooth, fast, and flowy? Is it mostly rideable? Are the challenges interesting, or will switchbacks and other trail elements bore you or make you sad—about yourself and your limited abilities? Will you want to occasionally whoop and holler with joy as you're riding? A 5 is *funnest ever*; 1 is lackluster *meh*.

SUFFERFEST FACTOR: Related to the Suffer Quotient, but with more poetic and emotional concerns included. Will it be hot? Lonely? Does the section take you on a busy road? Does the trail just plain suck? A 5 means it's freaking hard, ugly, non-singletracky, annoying. A score of 1 suggests an easy spin with little pain, physical or emotional.

PUCKER FACTOR: How scary is the ride? Is it exposed on steep terrain? Would a fall result in injury, death, or worse—damage to your bike? A 5 is scary as hell—a full pucker, if you will; a 1 is a ride without any sense of worry about endoing, crashing into trees and/or boulders, tumbling down cliffs, breaking collarbones, wrists, and other assorted skeletal parts, and so forth.

BEAUTY FACTOR: How pretty, majestic, and mesmerizing is the trail and surrounding landscape? Will you want to stop every 20 yards to take pictures and/or video, or will you be staring ten feet ahead of your front wheel the whole time because there's nothing great to look at? A 5 means some of the best sections of the CT, a landscape that will leave you breathless. A 1 would typically be boring, no vistas, bland trail, no wildflowers, dead gray trees, pretty lame, terribly monotonous, big yawn.

SUFFER QUOTIENT

This calculation adds a little more color to static data like total vertical and elevation outline. However, a Disclaimer: I took two semesters of calculus in college and got a C- that second semester. Which is to say, I am no mathematician, nor am I an expert on high-altitude physiology. But I am creative. And I'm well acquainted with misery, especially at high altitude.

So, let's do some math to determine how hard a day's ride is going to be.

Take Segment 23, for example. It's not far—a mere 21.9 miles. And the total vertical is around 3,500 feet—totally manageable, right?

Wrong!

Let's calculate the Suffer Quotient.

STEP 1

Calculate the vertical per mile: divide vertical feet of climbing by total mileage.

For Segment 23, you have
3,515 vertical / 21.9 miles = 160.5 feet of climbing per mile.

STEP 2

Determine median elevation above sea level.
If median elevation is not clearly stated anywhere, just take the lowest and highest elevation, add them together, and divide by 2.
For segment 23, low elevation is 11,938; highest is 12,991.

11,938 + 12,991 / 2 = median elevation of 12,464.
That's pretty freaking high.

STEP 3

Take your climbing-per-mile measure and multiply it by median elevation, and since this is a giant number, divide by 1,000.

So, for Segment 23
160.5 x 12,462 = 2,000,051. Divide by 1,000,
and you end up with a Suffer Quotient of 2,000.

For comparison, Segment 1 has 154 vertical feet per mile and a median altitude of 6,500.

154 x 6,500 = 1,001,000. Divide by 1,000
and you get a Suffer Quotient of 1,001.

You could then assume Segment 23 is twice as hard as Segment 1.
That seems about right. When you get there, you'll see.
Oh yes, you will most certainly see.

ABOVE Marshall Pass Top

PROSPECTIVE ITINERARY

As I've said, this itinerary closely matches my own and is merely a possible schedule. You're going to ride your ride, as you should. I do my best to tell the truths you need to know, things I wish I'd known when I was out there, with my bike, my earthy dad-bod, my exhaustion—truths unique to a mountain biker's perspective.

In general, a day's mileage varies according to ease of ride and quality—mostly, steepness of climbs. Big days on easy grades will eat up miles and vertical feet; shorter days will often include challenging terrain, brutal uphills, and lots of hike-a-bike. The day's Factor scores and Suffer Quotient will provide a clear sense of what lies ahead and will help you make informed decisions on how far and fast you might want to go.

Here's a quick summary, with one caveat: the mileage and vertical feet listed here are what I collected on my ride; often these numbers differed from what the *CT Guidebook* said, or what FarOut said. Your tracking system might also read things a little differently.

DAY 1: WATERTON CANYON TO LITTLE SCRAGGY (SEGMENTS 1 & 2)

SEGMENT 1 = 16.8 miles
SEGMENT 2 = 11.5
TOTAL = 28.3
VERTICAL = 2,830 + 2,482 = 5,312

DAY 2: LITTLE SCRAGGY TO TARRYALL (SEGMENT 3 + FIRST DETOUR)

SEGMENT 3 = 12.2 miles
LOST CREEK WILDERNESS DETOUR TO TARRYALL = 41
TOTAL = 53.2
VERTICAL = 1,975 + 4,163 = 6,138

DAY 3: TARRYALL TO JEFFERSON CREEK (SEGMENTS 5 & 6)

LOST CREEK DETOUR = 31 miles
SEGMENT 5 = 6.6
SEGMENT 6 = 6.0
TOTAL = 43.6
VERTICAL = 2,147 + 1,890 + 344 = 4,381

DAY 4: JEFFERSON CREEK TO BRECKENRIDGE (SEGMENT 6)

SEGMENT 6 = 26.7 miles
TO BRECKENRIDGE = 4.9
TOTAL = 31.6
VERTICAL = 3,680 + 381 = 4,061

DAY 5: BRECKENRIDGE TO GULLER CREEK (SEGMENTS 7 & 8)

BRECKENRIDGE TO GOLD HILL = 4.9 miles
SEGMENT 7 = 14.8
SEGMENT 8 = 5.2
TOTAL = 24.9
VERTICAL = 3,752 + 849 = 4,601

DAY 6: GULLER CREEK TO LEADVILLE (SEGMENTS 8 & 9 & HOLY CROSS/MT. MASSIVE DETOUR)

SEGMENT 8 = 20.2 miles
SEGMENT 9 = 2.5
HOLY CROSS/MT. MASSIVE DETOUR = 10
TOTAL = 32.7
VERTICAL = 3,870 + 150 + 405 = 4,425

DAY 7: LEADVILLE TO BUENA VISTA (DETOUR & SEGMENTS 11 & DETOUR)

MT. MASSIVE DETOUR (LEADVILLE) TO START OF SEGMENT 11 = 11 miles
SEGMENT 11 = 21.5 miles
END OF SEGMENT 12 TO BUENA VISTA = 19 miles
TOTAL = 51.5 miles
VERTICAL = 506 + 2,910 + 188 = 3,604

DAY 8: BUENA VISTA TO ANGEL OF SHAVANO (DETOUR & SEGMENTS 13 & 14)

BUENA VISTA TO SEGMENT 13 = 9 miles
SEGMENT 13 = 16.1 miles
SEGMENT 14 = 12.7
TOTAL = 37.8 miles
VERTICAL = 1,452 + 1,596 + 2,510 = 5,558

DAY 9: ANGEL OF SHAVANO TO MONARCH CREST TRAIL (SEGMENTS 14 & 15)

SEGMENT 14 = 5.3 miles
SEGMENT 15 = 10.3
TOTAL = 15.6
VERTICAL = 624 + 3,188 = 3,812

DAY 10: MONARCH CREST TRAIL TO SARGENTS MESA (SEGMENTS 15 & 16)

SEGMENT 15 = 9.0
SEGMENT 16 = 15.2
TOTAL = 24.2 miles
VERTICAL = 408 + 3,184 = 3,592

DAY 11: SARGENTS MESA TO LA GARITA DETOUR (SEGMENTS 17, 18, & DETOUR)

SEGMENT 17 = 20.4 miles
SEGMENT 18 = 13.8
LA GARITA DETOUR = 4.9
TOTAL = 39.1
VERTICAL = 2,810 + 1,259 = 4,069

DAY 12: LA GARITA DETOUR TO SPRING CREEK PASS (DETOUR & SEGMENT 22)

LA GARITA DETOUR = 52 miles
SEGMENT 22 = 3.3
TOTAL = 55.3
VERTICAL = 5,241 + 324 = 5,565

DAY 13: SPRING CREEK PASS TO CARSON SADDLE (SEGMENT 22)

SEGMENT 22 = 17.2 miles
VERTICAL = 3,505

DAY 14: CARSON SADDLE TO WEMINUCHE DETOUR (SILVERTON) (SEGMENT 23 & DETOUR)

SEGMENT 23 = 21.9 miles
SILVERTON DETOUR = 10.8
TOTAL = 32.7
VERTICAL = 3,515

DAY 15: WEMINUCHE DETOUR (SILVERTON) TO BOLAM PASS ROAD (CELEBRATION LAKE)

(DETOUR & SEGMENT 25)
WEMINUCHE DETOUR = 5.7 miles
SEGMENT 25 = 20.9
TOTAL = 26.6
VERTICAL = 1,582 + 3,799 = 5,381

DAY 16: BOLAM PASS ROAD TO BASE OF INDIAN TRAIL RIDGE CLIMB (SEGMENTS 26 & 27)

SEGMENT 26 = 10.9 miles
SEGMENT 27 = 12.3
TOTAL = 23.2
VERTICAL = 1,827 + 1,344 = 3,171

DAY 17: INDIAN TRAIL RIDGE TO JUNCTION CREEK TRAILHEAD (DURANGO)

(SEGMENTS 27 & 28)
SEGMENT 27 = 8.3 miles
SEGMENT 28 = 21.5
TO DURANGO = 3.5
TOTAL = 33.3
VERTICAL = 2,842 + 1,897 = 4,739

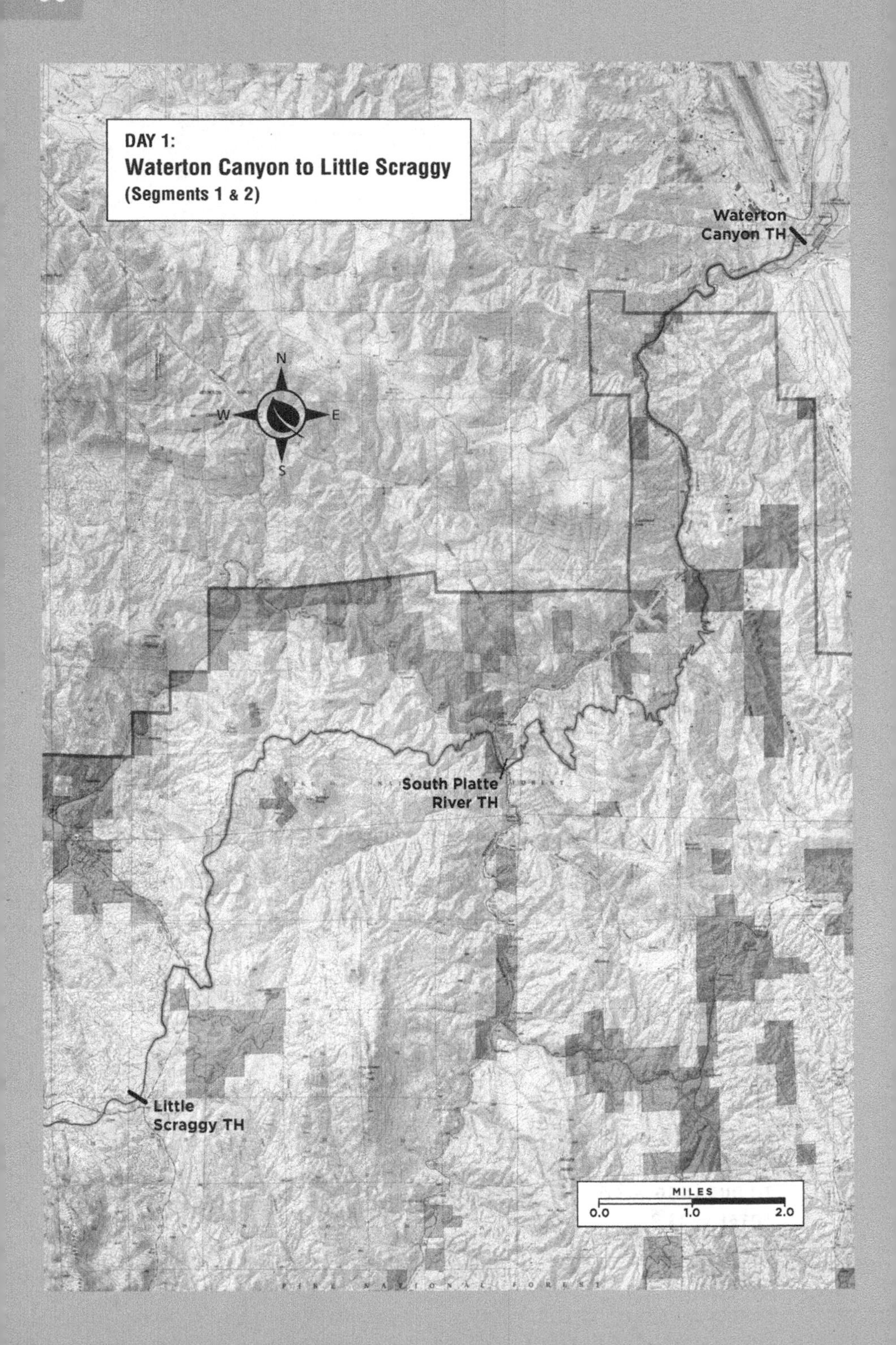
DAY 1:
Waterton Canyon to Little Scraggy
(Segments 1 & 2)
Waterton Canyon TH
N
W
E
S
South Platte River TH
Little Scraggy TH
MILES
0.0
1.0
2.0

DAY 1 WATERTON CANYON TO LITTLE SCRAGGY SEGMENTS 1 & 2

SEGMENT 1 = 16.8
SEGMENT 2 = 11.5
TOTAL = 28.3 miles
VERTICAL = 5,312 feet

FUN FACTOR: 4
It's your first day! That counts for a high fun score.

SUFFERFEST FACTOR: 3
Not too bad. You're just getting warmed up. Which is true, but also a pun: heat will be a factor.

PUCKER FACTOR: 2
Not very scary, but there are some loose patches.

BEAUTY FACTOR: 3
Pretty forests, Platte River, burn landscapes.

SUFFER QUOTIENT: 1,253

You're finally on your way! Can you believe it? Here's where all the months of planning and training, all the obsessing about gear and set-up and timing and weather forecasts fall away and it becomes simple: just pedal.

ABOVE Starting out, Waterton Canyon.

ABOVE First Colorado Trail Sign

After the essential and required photo of you and your bike next to the Waterton Canyon trailhead sign, the introductory road is long, smooth, and pretty quiet. If you're lucky, you'll see some bighorn sheep on the craggy canyon walls—or on the road itself, which lasts about six miles and provides a gentle transition away from the world of people, cars, pollution, noise, social media, and adult responsibilities. As you go deeper in, all that should begin to dissipate, and then you'll reach the turnout for the Strontia Springs Dam, the first of many impressive sights you're going to come across. Ahead lies the first bit of singletrack.

You'll spend most of your time on Segment 1 climbing. This is typical for the Denver metro foothills trails: you get on your bike, hit the trailhead, and then you climb, straight the hell up. For the most part it's rideable up to a bench at Lenny's Rest around eight miles in, and then you'll hit a series of ups and downs, some rideable, some not, some loose stretches, some tight switchbacks. Eventually, the trail runs along a stream and you'll slog your bike up a long series of natural rock steps. At times you'll feel like you're in a high alpine environment;

other times it will feel almost like a rain forest. You'll mostly be in the trees—ponderosa and lodgepole pine, some aspen. There won't be many majestic views. That happens on the next segment.

When you get close to the end of Segment 1, there's an awesome, really enjoyable downhill to the South Platte River and Gudy's Bridge. There's a parking lot there, most likely crowded with day-hikers and riders, a restroom, and the South Platte, which is a great place to restock on H2O. And you should—the next 12 miles will be hot with very little shade.

Segment 2 starts just across the river. You'll loop under the bridge, then cross a small scree field before beginning to climb. This one's a long one, but not too steep. The switchbacks, however, are hard—think tight turns, off-camber, and a loose, gravelly surface. Get used to that latter part—if there's one descriptor for Segment 2, it's this: kitty litter. It's like riding on tiny ball bearings, so be careful. With the added weight on your bike you can easily slide out, which, as you probably know from experience, only happens when you're going fast and having a really swell time.

Segment 2 is wicked slippery, but it's also gorgeous and surreal, coursing through the 1996 Buffalo Creek burn area. When you get close to the apex of the first climb, there are the remains of a cool little quartz mine, which provides a good place to stop for a quick rest or food intake. There are no trees for a while, and therefore no shade. You'll turn away from the mine and continue climbing, ending in a steep, short up. Massive rock formations dot the landscape; the trail winds in and out, up and down, and you'll be cruising along a flowy ribbon, whoopin' and hollerin' amidst the beauty of nature. It also

ABOVE Start of Segment 2.

tends to be deadly hot—especially in the afternoon if it's not cloudy or threatening rain. Hopefully you've procured enough water at the South Platte.

About halfway through the segment you'll enter a forest after passing a few large rock formations. The shade will be a welcome break from the sun, and yet, while there's not a long slog of a climb, there are many short punches and rollers, which will, as the day continues, begin to wear on your legs. Even so, it's mostly rideable and pretty fun.

Eventually you'll re-enter the burn area as you approach the last stretch of Segment 2. The trail flattens out for a few miles and it's an easy-going, rolling, twisty ride. It'll probably be getting late in the day when you'll see a few buildings in the distance, and then a roadway. This is close to the end of Segment 2. When you approach the roadway, don't make the left turn on the trail to the south just yet. One of the buildings you've spied is the well-known fire station with a water tap on its north side. Get on over there and fill up on H2O; you won't find another source for quite a while, and you'll want extra for cooking dinner and rehydrating. After you've resupplied, head on over to the Little Scraggy trailhead and parking lot. Once back on the trail, you'll immediately find lots of camping spots, but if there's still ample daylight and you're feeling good, you can crank out a few extra miles and camp farther in—maybe even in the midst of some of the bizarre granite formations that stand like sentinels all around.

And thus ends your first day on the Colorado Trail. Good work!

ABOVE Little Scraggy Rocks.

Rolling
Creek TH
Colorado Trail
560
DAY 2:
Little Scraggy to Tarryall
(Segment 3 & first detour)
560
211
77
211
N
W
E
S
Tarryall
77
MILES
0.0
1.0
2.0

DAY 2 LITTLE SCRAGGY TO TARRYALL SEGMENT 3 & FIRST DETOUR

SEGMENT 3 = 12.2 miles
LOST CREEK WILDERNESS DETOUR TO TARRYALL RESERVOIR = 54.1
TOTAL = 66.3
VERTICAL = 1,975 + 4,163 = 6,138

FUN FACTOR: 3.5
Scraggy is just plain fun.

SUFFERFEST FACTOR: 4
Mileage, and perhaps a headwind, will cause pain.

PUCKER FACTOR: 1
Not scary at all. Except maybe passing cars once you hit the pavement.

BEAUTY FACTOR: 2.5
It is beautiful, but compared to some of the other vistas . . .

SUFFER QUOTIENT: 937

Day 2 starts with the Little Scraggy Trail, and it's awesome. Like the end of the day before, it's fast and flowy, working in and out of massive, rounded rock formations, and rolling through several serene, wooded valleys. It's what the first day's riding would have been like if it weren't for the Buffalo Creek fire that denuded the area. Most if not all of it is rideable, and you'll be in the trees and have a little better traction. You should cover the distance fairly quickly.

About seven miles in, you'll begin climbing gently toward a complex of dirt roads, one of which eventually marks the Lost Creek Wilderness Detour. In general, all the Colorado Trail bike detours are long and a little boring, but they offer some nice scenery—and a break from the effort of riding, and walking, singletrack. This detour isn't so bad, but it'll take you awhile, so settle in.

The Lost Creek detour might be long and arduous, but it's also stunning. You'll be passing through another old burn area—the 2002 Hayman fire, one of the largest ever in the state of Colorado, started by a forlorn Forest Service employee who allegedly burned a letter sent to her by her estranged husband in a fire pit, but somehow the fire quickly got out of hand. More interesting rock formations, hills, and ridges. Lots of up and down. There also may be gun afficionados blasting some target practice off in the hills, which may generate an anxious vibe as you pedal away. The first part is dirt, gravel, and washboard; the second part is mostly roadway, with a bit more dirt road at the end. And yes, a few of the climbs really suck. You'll pass by Wellington Lake fairly early, and then there's a lot of meandering before you get to Tarryall Road, also known as County Road 77. It's a fair bit of climbing on small grades, so while you won't be busting a lung on every climb, eventually the effort will become obvious and you'll be pretty beat by the end of the day. And yes, it will likely be hot—and windy. Many riders have mentioned the wind as very deflating.

If you're following my camp schedule, your day will end near the Tarryall Reservoir, where you can grab a camp spot along the water, or close by, since it's first-come, first-serve and might be full. If you're feeling good and want to make it past the paved stuff, or if there's no place to stay at the Reservoir, you have about nine miles before you turn onto Park County Road 39, where there's easy-to-find camping. I've also heard that the Stagestop Saloon, just before the Road 39 turnoff, will often allow bikers to camp out back.

Or, screw all that noise and stress and just have a friend or significant other come pick you up at the start of the detour and drive you up to Kenosha.

ABOVE Lost Creek Detour Sign.

As I've said before, the Colorado Trail forces you to make a series of important binary decisions. Get to the Lost Creek Wilderness, and you can go left on the official detour, or you could go right, to Bailey, thereby saving yourself about 50 miles, but risking a rather sketchy climb up Highway 285? If you decide on the latter, here's where you'd break from the *Guidebook*, and go up SH 560 and then 550, which eventually turns into Route 68, to Bailey.

The first time I rode the CT I went right. I can't say it was a smart decision. (See below for the full story.)

Getting to 285 is no picnic in itself; there are a bunch of very steep pitches on the dirt roads toward Bailey. Once you get there, you can ride through some neighborhoods along 285 for a bit, up to a post office and the Shawnee Gathering Place, before you're dropped back onto the highway. Then the fun really starts. Highway 285 lacks a decent shoulder at many points. Traffic chugs along pretty damn fast and is riddled with RVs, trucks, and various other gas-chugging behemoths. If you're going to do this, try to get on the highway at a time when traffic is light—as in dawn. Be ready to occasionally stop and wait on the side of the road until traffic clears and you can race up the many shoulder-less stretches. Be ready for a powerful whoosh of air when vehicles fly past.

Also: it's a fairly steep climb up to Kenosha Pass where you'll reconnect with the CT, about 18 miles.

Other than all that, it's a real hoot! Just don't get flattened by an RV.

ABOVE Kenosha vista.

ABOVE Go this way.

NO TRAIL
PARKING

3 MY KENOSHA PASS STORY

I woke up around 6 a.m. at the Little Scraggy trailhead. It had rained overnight, but not enough to make things too soaked or muddy. I unzipped my screen, and then the moment of truth every camper experiences each and every morning: unzipping the exterior rain shell to see just what the heck is going on outside one's flimsy nylon abode. I was hoping to see dawn's rosy fingers gently touching the sky and the green forest around. You know, a scene that would make me want to kneel down and sing hosannas and such. But it wasn't quite like that.

The forest around me looked exactly the same as it did the night before. The trail waited, about 30 yards away, empty. The morning was cool and gray, almost misty. Everything was calm and quiet, almost creepily so.

I tried to be quick about things—I wanted to meet up with three dudes I'd met the day before so I could ride with them, hoping that would somehow protect me from getting obliterated by a semi—but my body was moving in slow motion. I was dragging. It seemed to take forever to eat my oatmeal breakfast, drink my instant coffee, and break camp. I didn't get on the trail until 7:30 a.m.

The trail was fast and fun—tacky and smooth, twisty and easy to roll, mostly flat or slightly downhill. I cruised. I hadn't been on this section of trail before, but certain points felt familiar, and that's always a comforting feeling.

LEFT & ABOVE: The top of Kenosha Pass. Get ready for some cruising.

At one point, I entered a large open space overhung with trees. Everything was so green, it was very lovely. A woman runner approached, the first person I'd seen all morning. I pulled off the trail to let her pass. She was moving at a good pace. As she got near, we exchanged salutations, and then she stopped and stared at me.

"Aren't you Mike Henry from Lighthouse?" she asked.

Of all the things to happen on a cool Monday morning in the middle of literally nowhere. It's not like I'm famous or anything, but I do know lots of people from my job as director of a place called Lighthouse Writers Workshop, a literary arts center in Denver. I teach writing workshops there in addition to running the place, which my wife and I founded in 1997. Speaking of long, incredible journeys—building Lighthouse has certainly been one. It's been a ton of work, but it's been an amazing ride, no pun intended. I couldn't have asked for a better work life, a more rewarding career, than the one I have.

"Uh yeah, I am Mike Henry."

"I've taken a bunch of workshops at Lighthouse. In fact, my daughter just finished youth camp there last week."

I thanked her for being part of the Lighthouse community. We commiserated on the weirdness of running into each other in such circumstances, and I told her I was planning on riding a fair amount of the Colorado Trail, hoping to get to Leadville in a week, and that I'd ride the rest next summer. "But man, it's slow going," I said.

"Good luck!" she said. And then she was off like a fox.

Back to the trail. Pedaling. Carefully, painfully, slowly. Attempting to conserve my quads from overworking themselves.

The funny thing about riding like this is that your heart rate doesn't really go crazy high—especially if you've properly trained (for that, see Getting Ready section of this book); I think for the most part my heart rate stayed well in the lower aerobic range—about 120 to 140 beats per minute. You just can't max yourself out when you're riding eight or more hours per day. I used to be good at this when I was a runner. I understood the meaning behind LSD—*long slow distance*—where you take it easy and don't overtax yourself. It's a prime rule of endurance training and racing—stay within yourself. I remember a world-class runner, a woman we were training with in high school at cross country camp. Our camp—a really big house, really—sat on the shore of a small lake, and the final day our task was to run around this lake, about nine miles total. She said, "You should finish your LSD runs feeling like you could go do it all over again. If you go any faster than that, you're going too hard."

I kept the runner's advice in mind as I climbed a long series of switchbacks, sometimes sliding off the bike and pushing it uphill. Still, though I felt some urgency. I needed to meet up with my dudes, both for comfort and traffic safety. I kept an eye out for tents and bikes leaning against trees, but saw nothing. My hopes began to dim as I got closer and closer to the decision point: crossing a dirt-road that marked the beginning of the 70-mile Lost Creek work-around. Once I got there, I'd have to decide: go left and do the full work-around, or go right and hump nine miles into Bailey and then onto 285.

Well, I got there, and almost crashed, spectacularly. The trail crossed a dirt road; but the last ten feet or so, it dropped precipitously and I picked a steeper line than I should have. I had a moment to think to myself: *You're going to endo. You're going to break your neck and die out here, where there's no one around. You are stupid and foolish.*

Somehow the physics of my front fork travel and size of my wheels—29 inches, thank you very much—landed hard in the crevasse and pushed back, keeping me upright.

I pulled into the parking lot for the Lost Creek Wilderness and checked out the billboard, read the maps. There were three cars in the lot, but human beings were non-existent. My riding dudes were nowhere to be found.

For some reason, bikes are not allowed in Wilderness areas. The Colorado Trail travels through no less than five of these areas, which bikers have to work around. Oh, how I wished I could keep riding the Trail! I didn't want to slog the 70 miles of the detour, nor did I want to ride into Bailey and try to ride up 285 all by myself.

I ate a Clif bar and sucked down a gel pack. I girded my loins and went right, toward Bailey. Highway 285, and almost certain death by truck, here I come.

The worst thing about this section of dirt road was how it went up. And down. And then up. Then down. The rolling hills broke my spirit. Every time I thought I'd made the last climb, another one appeared around the bend. I had to stop and suck wind periodically. I got into the habit of taking four long, deep breaths before clipping back in and cranking away.

After about an hour of this, the road turned to asphalt. There was a crew at one point, out in the middle of nowhere, repaving a section of road, complete with a stop-sign guy to control the invisible traffic. It was kind of surreal. The smell of fresh tar filled my nostrils. I kind of liked it.

I got to the little town of Bailey, Colorado (population 8,189) and found a shop and diner that sold cowboy hats, jewelry, tourist t-shirts, and diner food. I know, it had only been a day or so, but I was definitely craving real food. I ordered a large coffee and a poppy-seed muffin. And then a Sprite and a BLT. With fries. I sat at a small table inside the shop, close to a long bar, and scarfed down the food while reading the colorful history of the place, originally a saloon, printed on the back of the laminated menu.

I was sitting in the back of the store and couldn't see outside, so when I opened the front door and found that it was raining, I was a little surprised. I was fully prepared to ride in the rain—on the trail. But on a busy road in the rain? This road, in particular? My tired muscles twinged with the beginnings of low-grade panic.

I sat on a bench outside the restaurant and watched the rain fall. An endless stream of cars, trucks, and RVs hissed by. After about an hour, I walked over to a gas station and bought some chips and other garbage food, which I scarfed down. The rain gradually let up, but the clouds to the west didn't look happy. I decided to give it a go.

When you're alone, with no one to talk to—except for that voice inside your head, part parent, part logistician, part berator-in-chief, part insane person—fear can transform you. Fear can make you super-focused. It can turn you into a machine of perfection. It can make you do things you never thought you could. It can also turn you into a stressed-out, scared shell of a person. Sometimes both.

ABOVE Lunch, anyone?

When I started up 285, it could have gone either way. I seriously contemplated what it would be like to die out on the non-existent shoulder of this road, clobbered by a semi or 40-foot-long RV. I wondered what sort of *memento mori* my wife and kids would install at the specific location of my obliteration. Would there be a bouquet of faded plastic flowers? A Clash poster? A vinyl record, like *Exile on Main Street*? Elvis Presley figurine in gold jacket? A sad, laminated poem?

My senses were dialed in. My balance, perfect. My pedal strokes, definitive and strong.

It began to pour. And then a semi blasted by me and the wind shear and backsplash pushed me off the road into the weedy ditch and I almost crashed.

I pulled the bike up under a large pine tree about 20 feet off the road to wait it out, but the rain picked up. The temperature, already not very comfortable, plummeted. I pulled out my tent rain-cover and huddled under it, my ass aching as I sat on a boulder.

I remained there for about two hours. The rain showed no signs of letting up. I began to shiver. My fingers turned pruney and white.

I thought about a lot of things. I thought about my life. I thought about those who raised me but are gone now—my mother and, more recently, her parents, my Non and Pop. I thought about my sisters, all four of them. I thought about my wife, my kids, the dog. What a lucky life I've led. How I couldn't have asked for one as fine and lovely. I thought about my freezing toes and fingers. A litany of things, really, to no great depth—this wasn't a time for epiphanies. (Those would come later in the trip.) More like an afternoon of cataloging. All the time, Bob Dylan's voice in my head singing "A Hard Rain's Gonna Fall" and then Patti Smith's voice, singing the same song at Dylan's Nobel Prize ceremony.

Most of the time I was completely ensconced under the rain tarp. Occasionally, I pulled it back a little to see how the rain was doing. Each time it was doing just fine, thank you very much. Nature didn't care about me sitting here under a tree, freezing in a hard rain. It didn't care that I wanted to get to Kenosha Pass. Why would it?

I couldn't sit there forever, and I definitely wasn't going to ride 285 in such conditions. So, when I looked out from under my tarp one more time, I spied a small sign up the road. It read: Bailey Lodge.

Bailey Lodge wasn't too far, but I had to ride on the road again for about 200 yards, no small feat. I waited until the traffic cleared and humped it over there as fast as I could, my thighs twinging and aching.

I pulled my bike under an awning and tried to figure out which door was the office because there was no sign. The Bailey Lodge is basically a two-story motel, so I had a long line of doors to choose from. One didn't have a number, and I was about to try the knob when, from another room, a severe-looking blonde-haired women wearing a long, flowered dress appeared. (Sister-wife is the descriptor that came to mind.) I asked after a room; she nodded and opened the door I was about to try and motioned me in. She was barefoot and didn't say a word. Another woman appeared and checked me in. I went to my room, promptly stripped down and took the hottest, longest, most blissful shower that humankind has ever known. I emptied my gear and hung it on the furniture to dry. I curled up under the bedcovers and took a nap. When I woke, I microwaved some water and ate a very disgusting freeze-dried meal—there was no way I was going to go back out into that damn rain to get food.

Eventually, the sky outside darkened into night, but the rain refused to let up.

Can I fully express what a good idea that room was, how happy I was to be in there, warm and dry? Probably not. If I had met up with those dudes, I'd be somewhere past Kenosha Pass, probably on my way toward Jefferson Creek, which has a campground where I once stayed, years ago. I would be in the rain—a cold, steady rain.

I'm all for a rugged, rustic experience, but I'm also 50 years old. And I have a credit card.

Swaddled in bed, I watched the newest *Game of Thrones*—the Loot Train episode—on my iPhone. I fell asleep at 8:30 p.m., and slept—not like the proverbial baby, because babies don't sleep very well at all, everyone knows that—but like a tired old man who's ridden his bike way too far.

I woke up at 5 a.m. hoping to get on the road early, before traffic got too bad. In other words: so that I might not die.

I climbed onto the bike at 5:45 a.m., just as a golden dawn was breaking over the mountains to the east. The sky was a clear Colorado blue that always makes me happy, but it was cold. I wore pretty much every single piece of clothing I had—except for my bedtime boxer shorts. When I checked my weather app, it said the temp was 42 degrees.

In this brisk, clean air, I pedaled up a side road, filled with cute houses and meadows populated by horses and mule deer. Dew clung to the grasses, silvery in the early light. Gradually my stiff legs warmed up and a small glimmer of hope bloomed in my heart. Maybe I'll do okay on this whole ride thing. Maybe I won't get hit by a truck, after all.

That good feeling lasted about 20 minutes, disappearing when I turned onto the highway and began the real slog up Kenosha Pass.

Overall, traffic was light. Until it wasn't. Cars and trucks came in waves—the way things typically work when you're on a winding two-lane road and can't pass slower cars easily. Vehicles tend to cluster together, and I did well to pull over those times when such a train approached and ahead there wasn't an easy out. I spent lots of time waiting in driveways and ditches, hopping back onto the thin, white line when things cleared, pedaling like a maniac.

I got into a decent rhythm doing this, focusing on the white line. Ah the stable, unending, unbroken line leading me to my destiny: the top of the mountain. Only once did a huge truck blast by me, the wind knocking me off the line, though I was able to stay aboard my trusty Stumpjumper.

The problem with long slow climbs, though, is this: you end up staying in the seat for extended periods of time. And I hadn't done a ton of super-long rides while training for this sojourn. Which is to say: my butt began to ache like it's never ached before. I can't really describe it, but it's a dull pain that radiates from your behind—remember, the official term is *sitbones* or *ischial tuberosity*, if you want to be fancy—up your back, down your hips to your knees, and into your business. (You know what I mean.) Things usually go numb after a while, which is even worse, because this—at least for me—is accompanied by yet another slow drip of panic. What if feeling never returns?

Stopping and getting out of the saddle was the only salve to ease the pain. I wasn't going to climb while standing on the pedals—my quads would surely not deal with such stupidity. So, I rode. And stopped. And rode some more. And stopped. I made it to a teeny plaza area just before the bricked-up Roberts Tunnel outlet and sat in front of an abandoned storefront and ate a Clif Bar. It was still early—around 7:30 a.m. I'd been climbing for well over an hour. My feet, which were totally frozen, warmed up a bit, but only after I took off my shoes and vigorously rubbed my toes. Feeling gradually returned to various extremities. And then I rode on.

Like lots of mountain passes and many long, gradual climbs, you think you're getting close to the top only to be tricked by what's called a "false summit." Here's what Wikipedia has to say about this term:

> In mountaineering, a **false** peak or **false summit** is a peak that appears to be the pinnacle of the mountain but upon reaching, it turns out the **summit** is higher. **False** peaks can have significant effects on climber's psychological state by inducing feelings of dashed hopes or even failure.

Amen on that last sentence.

One other item from my extensive web research on this term: Elevation Beer Company, located in Poncha Springs, Colorado, near

Salida and the Colorado Trail, has a beer called *False Summit.* It comes in a bottle with a champagne cork in it, which I think is a little bit fancy for a bottle of beer, and therefore it very much intrigues me. Also intriguing: it has 11% alcohol, and, according to Elevation Beer's website, "notes of caramel, oak and dark Belgian candi sugar." Needless to say, visiting their tasting room is on my someday-to-do list.

Anyway, back to 285 and actual false summits. There were several. And after each one, the road seemed to steepen. Maybe that was only me and my slowly leaking-away energy and positivity. I knew this entire trip would be a slog, but I didn't realize my emotions would be so bipolar. One moment I'm feeling great, singing Beatles songs to myself, pedaling away, gradually eating up miles, and five minutes later everything hurts, cars are careening past, inches away from my left elbow, and I want to pull over and cry, I want to call my wife and tell her to come pick me up, this was a stupid idea and I am going to sell my stupid bike and take up golfing and stand-up paddle-boarding.

But I kept going. It's the only thing I really know how to do. I ran cross country and track through high school and college. I once ran a five-mile road race in a little over 25 minutes, and finished the Boston Marathon in a little over 3 hours. I can suffer mightily—making little circles with both feet, pedal stroke after pedal stroke. I can do that. Physically, and mentally, I feel like I've experienced lots of difficult things—many forms of loss—but I've kept on. I've endured. I am one stubborn son-of-a-bitch.

So forget quitting. I will never quit. Even if I can't feel my junk. Or my toes.

When the road opened up a little, with pretty meadows on either side, I knew I was close. I stopped one more time to let the seat-pain subside, caught my breath, and ventured on. And then, out of nowhere, a big, green sign: Kenosha Pass Trailhead. I'd made it! It was sunny and I was alive. None of the 178 cars—I'd counted them as they careened past—had run me over.

I leaned my bike up against a parking sign and stretched my legs. I removed my jacket and basked in the sun, even though the breeze was strong and still cold. A few hikers entered the trail, which begins in a dense aspen forest, so it's a little like entering a long, winding hallway. I ate a bunch of food—my second breakfast—a term from *Lord of the Rings,* if you don't know. My youngest daughter and I had been reading the trilogy together for quite a long while, and before I'd left for this ride, Frodo and Sam had just entered Mordor. The commonalities were not lost on me. But my task was surely not as grim as theirs. Right?

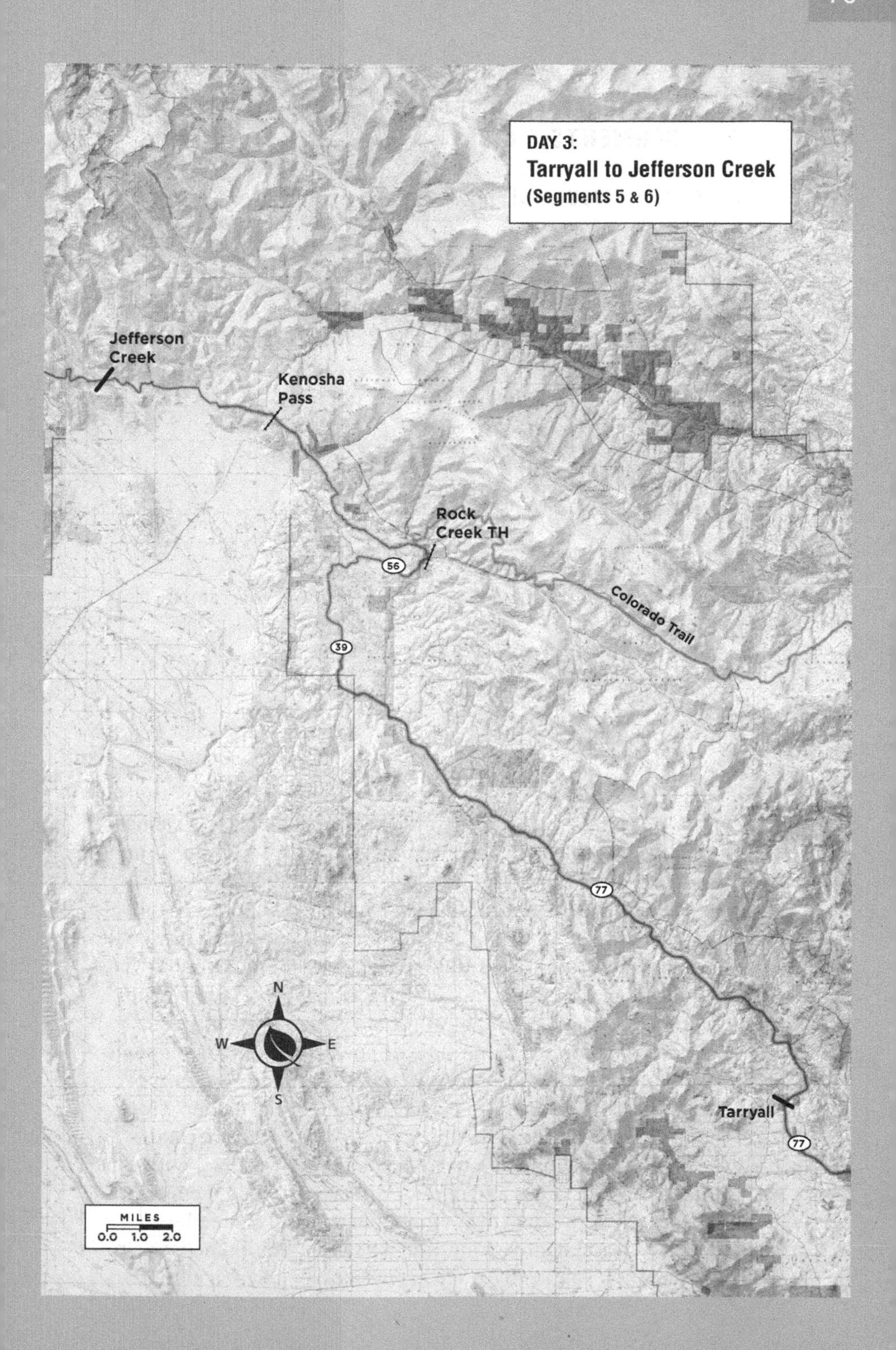
DAY 3:
Tarryall to Jefferson Creek
(Segments 5 & 6)
Jefferson Creek
Kenosha Pass
Rock Creek TH
56
Colorado Trail
39
77
N
W
E
S
Tarryall
77
MILES
0.0 1.0 2.0

DAY 3 TARRYALL TO JEFFERSON CREEK SEGMENTS 5 & 6

LOST CREEK DETOUR = 31 miles
SEGMENT 5 = 6.6
SEGMENT 6 = 6.0
TOTAL = 43.6
VERTICAL = 2,147 + 1,890 + 344 = 4,381

FUN FACTOR: 4
You feel a little like a roadie. Plus, it's fun to connect Buff Creek to Kenosha.

SUFFERFEST FACTOR: 3
Mostly, it's just a slog.

PUCKER FACTOR: 2
If there's a lot of traffic, a higher score might be warranted.

BEAUTY FACTOR: 4
Wilderness detour is pretty cool.

SUFFER QUOTIENT: 956

If you've gone the way of the official detour, the roadie climbs waiting for you this morning aren't too brutal, and you should have a chance to get warmed up and shake off the fatigue you'll most likely be feeling. Today's route will feel different, for sure. Once you're done with the road part of the detour, you'll be entering big mountains, finally done with the dry, hot foothills, inching your way close to a first high alpine crossing at Georgia Pass. But before you get there, you'll want to stop at the Stagestop Store and Saloon and maybe get some grub and resupply. It's a classic kind of Colorado eatery—lots of western character and good food in the middle of nowhere. Then there's some more road with a decent shoulder, which is nice, before you turn off CR 77 and onto CR 39 somewhere after mile 60 of the detour. More dirt road, and then you reach the Rock Creek Trailhead at a small parking lot. The trail from here to Kenosha is very rideable, with vistas that expand for miles and miles—classic Colorado mountain biking. It starts with a fairly long climb, but the trail should be all yours until you begin approaching Kenosha Pass. You'll know you're getting close when you begin to see groups of day hikers and touristy types—i.e. older gentlemen in white sneakers from Costco and dad-jeans, plus kids, dogs, and whatnot.

You'll cross Highway 285 and then the ride enters a new ecosystem—the trail on this side of Kenosha Pass is rolling, fun, often fast, in the midst of pine and aspen trees, all very rideable. The views to South Park and beyond are vast. Eventually the singletrack bottoms out in a series of meadows, and then you'll cross a rustic footbridge over Jefferson Creek. Nearby there's a campground with restrooms.

There are lots of camping spots as part of the campground, but most likely they'll be reserved. Look for a free spot along the creek; there are plenty. If you're feeling good, however, by all means begin the climb to Georgia Pass. There's good camping in multiple spots. And getting a few extra miles in will shorten tomorrow's jaunt to Breckenridge, which'll maximize your lounging around, restauranting, and resupply time before getting back on the trail at Gold Hill. If you're really serious, you could skip Breck altogether and see if you can get up and over the Tenmile Range before settling in around Copper Mountain, where there are also restaurants, beds, and resupply opportunities available.

ABOVE Lost Creek Detour.

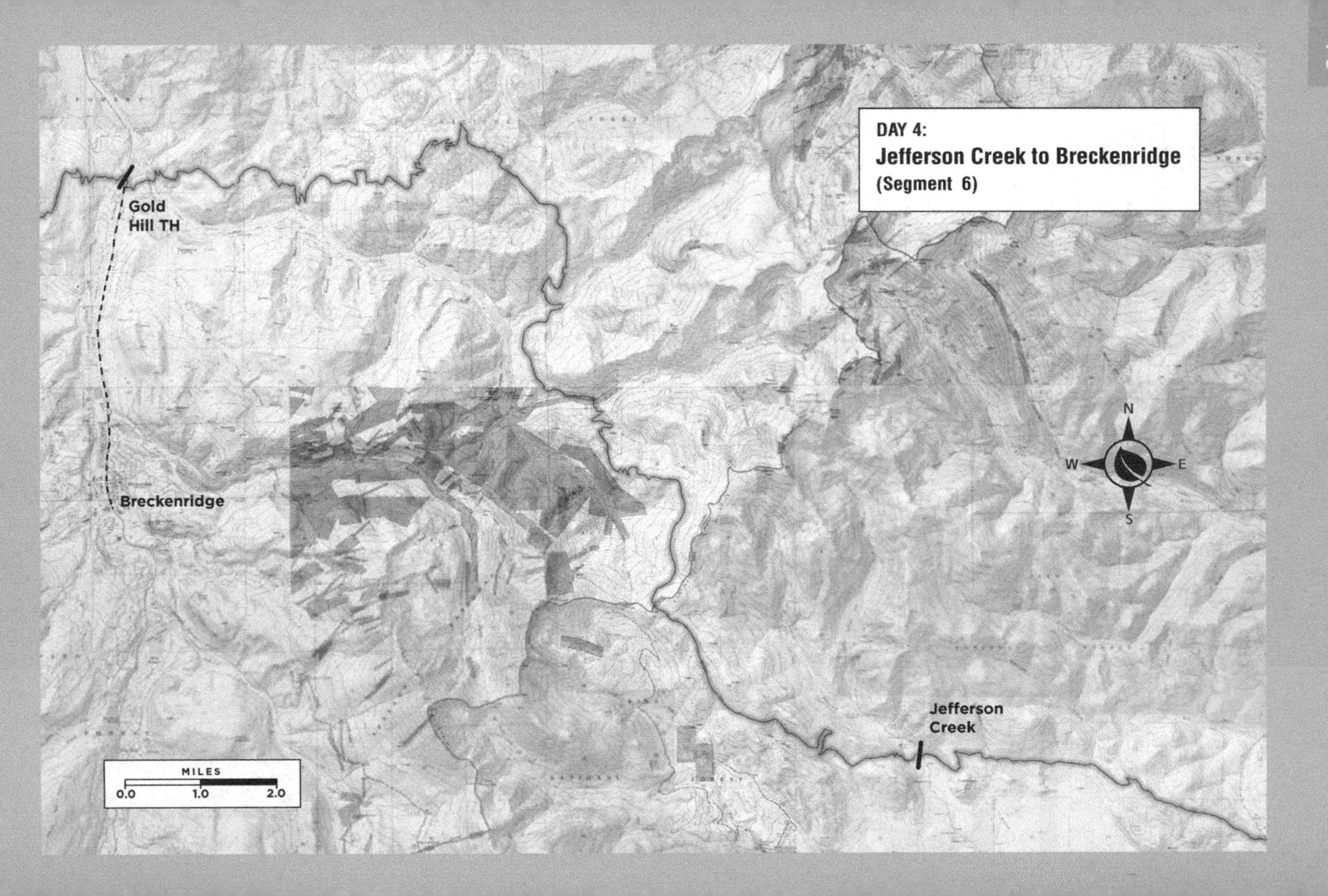
DAY 4:
Jefferson Creek to Breckenridge
(Segment 6)
Gold
Hill TH
Breckenridge
N
W
E
S
Jefferson
Creek
MILES
0.0
1.0
2.0

DAY 4 JEFFERSON CREEK TO BRECKENRIDGE SEGMENT 6

SEGMENT 6 = 26.7 miles
TO BRECKENRIDGE = 4.9
TOTAL = 31.6
VERTICAL = 3,680 + 381 = 4,061

FUN FACTOR: 3.5
Nice rolling singletrack, some slow, some very fast.

SUFFERFEST FACTOR: 3
It's a long stretch of sitting and climbing, but not too terrible.

PUCKER FACTOR: 1
Except for switchbacks by Tiger Run Resort—those are 4.

BEAUTY FACTOR: 3
If you live in Colorado, you'll be seeing some familiar views as you near Breckenridge.

SUFFER QUOTIENT: 1,354

In the morning, you should be pretty darn excited, since you could soon be in Breckenridge and all the trappings of civilization: namely, food, beer, and a warm bed if you choose to get a room in town. The trail starting out is rocky and steep in sections, but I found it super-rideable, which helped boost my confidence and gave me a nice jolt of energy.

Overall, the climb to Georgia Pass is long, but not overwhelming—it's more of a sit-and-pedal-and-zone-out kind of ride. Eventually you'll reach a really cool lookout point and might think you're close to the top of the pass, but alas, it isn't true. There's a rooty, rocky stretch and then you settle in for the final push to get above treeline.

I don't think I'll ever get bored climbing to treeline and the exhilaration that washes over me when I reach the top of a Colorado high-country trail. Georgia Pass is no exception. It's maybe not as remote as some of the other high places you'll cross over on your sojourn, but no matter. It's often nice to share the moment with perfect strangers, someone to witness your accomplishment. High fives and compliments should be doled out aplenty.

Georgia Pass is very pretty—and high, topping out at 11,598. (Later on, this will be a relatively low elevation, I kid you not.) Breathe deep, get all that O2 in the blood. Take in the views from the

Continental Divide, with Mount Guyot looming to the west. And then, when you're ready, enjoy the cruise down. The beginning is sweet singletrack and then it gets a little rocky—a great chance to show off your tech skills, or downhill hike-a-bike skills. Either one's good. After that, you'll spend a good portion of time on rolling terrain, so pace yourself. There are several creek crossings, too.

When I rode this part, at one point I spied several rustic buildings off in the woods. As I got closer, a huge fenced-in pen with a pack of wolves, or maybe wolf-hybrids, appeared, and they began howling away. I might have howled my own return greeting.

Eventually the trail hooks up with the Keystone Resort network, flowing in and out of beetle-kill forests before opening up into some very pretty greenspaces, and then, probably when you're getting pretty sick of yet another punchy climb, the trail reaches civilization and devilishly zig-zags down into the Tiger Run resort along Route 9, along which there's a paved bike-path that can take you into Breckenridge. You can choose to be lazy and wait for the free shuttle into town, if you like. For serious riders and misanthropes who wish to eschew the trappings of civilization in a touristy mountain town, you'll cross Route 9 for the trailhead to Segment 7 and the Gold Hill trail. There's plenty of camping up by Miner's Creek if you're planning on spending the night on this side of the Tenmile Range. If not, you've got a very serious climb ahead of you—a robust mix of riding and hiking. If the weather is sketchy, or if it's getting late, you'll want to stop here and rest up for tomorrow's big day.

ABOVE Jefferson Creek Bridge.

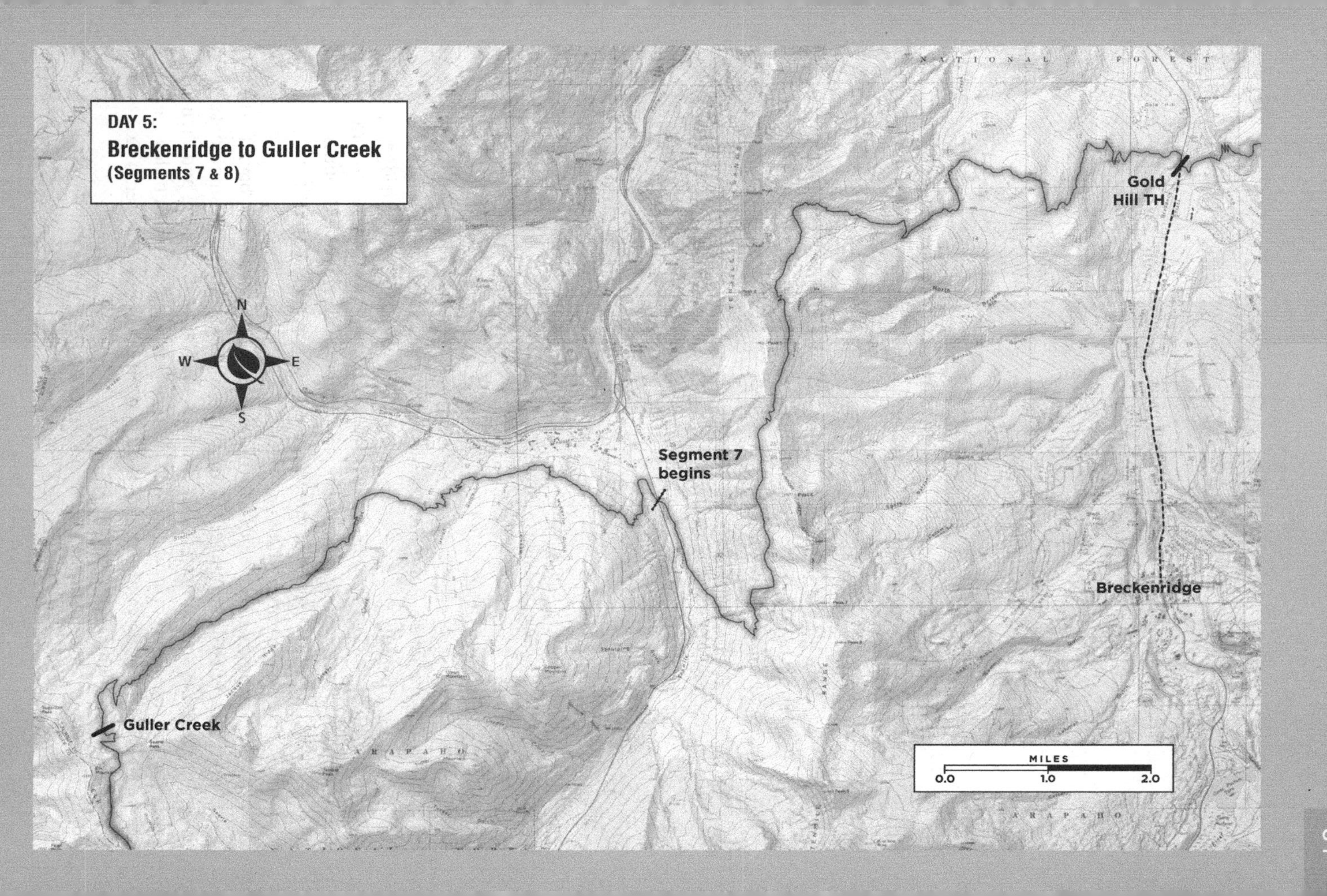
DAY 5:
Breckenridge to Guller Creek
(Segments 7 & 8)
N
W
E
S
NATIONAL FOREST
Gold
Hill TH
Segment 7
begins
Breckenridge
Guller Creek
MILES
0.0
1.0
2.0

DAY 5 BRECKENRIDGE TO GULLER CREEK SEGMENTS 7 & 8

BRECKENRIDGE TO GOLD HILL = 4.9 miles
SEGMENT 7 = 14.8
SEGMENT 8 = 5.2

TOTAL = 24.9 miles
VERTICAL = 3,752 + 849 = 4,601 feet

FUN FACTOR: 4
It's pretty cool to see how close Copper and Breckenridge actually are to one another. Plus, the descent into Copper is tremendous.

SUFFERFEST FACTOR: 5
It's not a lot of miles, but there's a brutally steep hike-a-bike to the crest of the Tenmile Range. Probably one of the steepest stretches of the entire Colorado Trail.

PUCKER FACTOR: 4
Some steep drop-offs at various points. Weather could be really scary if you're not careful.

BEAUTY FACTOR: 4
Grand views from the top of the Tenmile Range. Also, Guller Creek is super purdy.

SUFFER QUOTIENT: 2,004

If you were smart—or a cheater, depending on your point of view about trail-riding purity—and stayed somewhere in Breckenridge, you'll have lots of options for breakfast. In other words: you have the opportunity to eat real food. I highly recommend Daylight Donuts, which has a full breakfast menu. Be sure to grab a few wheels of deliciousness to take with you.

Once you've scarfed down your fill, ride the paved trail back north to the Gold Hill Trailhead. Or, if you're like me, feel just a small dose of guilt as you hop onto the free shuttle that takes you there, and then let the internal recriminations go. You're traveling 500-plus miles on a bike for crying out loud, and today you'll cross over the Tenmile Range, which is no joke.

On my trip, I stayed in a Breck hotel and slept deep in a soft, cozy bed while outside it rained, hard, most of the night. I can't fully

ABOVE This is where you're headed.

describe the relief I felt when I woke up in the early dawn, warm and groggy, and heard the pitter-pat of rain on the hotel's rooftop. Sure, my tent probably would have held up, but if previous experience is any guide, a slow, agonizing drip would have plopped right in the middle of my forehead all night long.

About the Gold Hill trail: It begins as a gradual climb in a wide, open meadow that's been mostly denuded of trees. The climb is no big deal—if the trail is dry. If it's rained, the trail is a muck-fest. You'll end up walking, but not on the trail; even unweighted tires will pick up enough mud to seize your wheels. This was my experience, and it sucked.

After about three miles, the trail climbs over a rounded hill and meanders back and forth over Miner's Creek. Eventually it enters remnants of the Gold Hill burn, which devastated the area in 2017. When I went through, the fire had recently been put out; there were thousands of blackened, branchless lodgepole pine trunks, like stubble on a giant's face. Large boulders had split in the heat. Sections of the trail had been washed out, and makeshift detours had been hastily patched together. Altogether, the landscape had a haunted, charred beauty to it.

Past the burn area, it gets steep. And then steeper. As in multiple unrideable sections. Lots of baby-heads and mini-headwalls. The numbered peaks of the Tenmile Range become visible, but don't bother

ABOVE The Gold Hill burn area.

trying to figure out how you're going to get over them—from this vantage they're a wall of rock with no clear crossing point.

For a small bit, about four miles in, the trail flattens out and rolls through a narrow meadow fed by the uppermost reaches of Miner's Creek. You've again reached the high alpine quiet of Colorado mountains. Wildflowers abound, the stream whispers peacefully, and the gray cragginess of Peak 5 looms in the distance. This section is fairly rideable.

As you get closer to Peak 5 however, the trail ticks up yet again. It's very hard. Eventually, you gain treeline and the narrow saddle you'll eventually traverse appears to your left. There are large rock stands that are home to various pika and marmot, and the view back to the east will stop you short: Lake Dillon shimmering in the distance, as well as the mountains you crossed to get here. This is a great place to hang out and have some lunch or a snack, but don't wait too long—there's still a fair bit of work to do before you reach Copper Mountain. If you do take a break, be sure to say hello to some of the pika that live there in the rocks. They are super cute.

For the last push, the trail zig-zags up and over a saddle, and it's maybe 400 yards or so, but it'll take some time because you'll be walking. Well, not actually walking—it's more like inch-worming: push the bike forward until your arms are straight; lock your brakes so the bike doesn't slide backwards; take two or three steps to catch

ABOVE A pretty little Miner's Creek meadow before some exceptionally steep hike-a-bike.

up. Then repeat. And repeat. And breathe. It may seem impossible, but you can do this. This is where your wintertime weight-lifting training regimen of shoulder presses and squats will come in handy.

Didn't do any of those types of workouts? That's a shame, a damn shame. Didn't you read the chapter on how to prepare? Don't you remember the equation for power from high school physics? Power = Work / Elapsed Time. More power converts to less time.

Once you make it to the saddle, the views open up even more as the trail crosses into Breckenridge ski area, but don't be fooled. I had the naïve belief that once I reached the top of the saddle it would be all downhill into Copper. That's not how it goes. You traverse from Peak 5 to Peak 6, and the route here a ribbon of rocky singletrack that's very narrow and exposed, and drops off steeply. To be honest, I got a little freaked out and walked much of this part, though someone with more guts and determination will probably ride it no problem.

Along those lines, here's where you might want to give yourself a little pep talk. You *can* ride most of this section. It won't be easy—sure, it's narrow and tricky and cuts across a steep slope—but the trail grade isn't too bad. Then again, if you're conserving energy and want to stay safe, just walk it. Riding won't be much faster. The little stones littering the trail are a real pain in the ass. The only issue with walking, though is this: the trail is so narrow that you have to be ever-aware of the pedal sticking out where you're trying to walk, so that you don't consistently whack your shin or calf against it. It's exceptionally frustrating, and I never really did figure out a way to avoid it when walking on narrow singletrack. Tall socks helped a little bit, but I still ended up with a multitude of gashes and bruises.

At about eight miles in, you come to a really cool threshold: Breckenridge ski area is on your left; Copper Mountain and Vail are to the west and on your right, and some very high mountains, like Mount Holy Cross, beckon. This is the Trail's high-point along the Tenmile Range, at 12,495 feet. If you see any storms looming in the distance, I advise you to skedaddle down the mountain. There's absolutely no protection up there. Even if the weather is good, it'll most likely be windy.

Once you cross over, the downhill is, to put it simply, awesome. Fast, steep, and tacky, it bombs down into the woods above Copper Mountain and Route 91, which leads up to Fremont Pass. Some of the switchbacks are a little tight, so stay in control. You'll make up lots of time here; enjoy yourself! (Here's where I saw a relatively rare thing in the wilderness: a bare behind. A woman was changing into a pair of long pants and didn't hear me descending. She was with a large group, and apologized, laughing about it; I said there was nothing to apologize for—such is life on the Colorado Trail.)
There's something joyous about coming back into civilization again, even if you've only been out in the wilds for a day or even an afternoon, and that's how coming into Copper Mountain feels. Relief,

ABOVE Copper Mountain, your destination, off in the stormy distance.

happiness, a sense of accomplishment at having slogged over one of the more challenging sections of the CT. You've run the classic course of the Hero's Journey. You've climbed into the wilderness and down into the depths of your soul. You have returned to tell your story to the people, those good folks at Copper Mountain Ski Resort, who may be:

a. A very nice and chatty older couple from Oklahoma/Texas/North Carolina lounging in chairs by the fire pit;

b. A lithe, chill person (obviously a serious rider) at the bike shop or waiter at a restaurant;

c. Your loved ones via cell phone.

When I finally reached Copper I was pretty spent, but the downhill had boosted my endorphins and I was feeling pretty blissful. I bought some bottled water and a couple of candy bars at a corner store in the shiny-new manufactured mountain town, and settled into a table at a restaurant that overlooked the base area carnival/playground/county fair. If you've ever been to a ski area in the summer you know what I mean: cool tunes in the air, playing from stereo speakers disguised as rocks; a jumpy-bungee-cord-trampoline apparatus with children flying around, most likely acquiring a good case of whiplash; a miniature golf course; a small stream and meadow adorned with Adirondack chairs; downhill riders catching big air, then settling onto the high-speed chairlift to take them back up the mountain for another run.

The restaurant meal I consumed—a plate of Buffalo wings, a giant salad with bacon bits, three glasses of Sprite, and a frothy, cold IPA—filled my belly and all was good. It began to rain a little, though much of the sky remained blue. I knew there was a rainbow somewhere, but didn't feel the need to find it.

Leaving Copper Mountain can be bittersweet then. You can't camp at the ski area, so it's either backtracking to Tenmile Creek (and the highway) or continuing on for a bit. I recommend the latter. The ride is easy and rolls through a lovely Colorado alpine forest, crossing various ski trails and service roads before you leave the ski area boundary and enter wilderness again. The trail is smooth, the forest hasn't been decimated by pine beetles (yet), and you'll be farther toward the long climb to Kokomo and Searle passes. I highly recommend several comfortable campsites along Guller Creek with some really pretty views, just before the climb to Searle Pass begins in earnest.

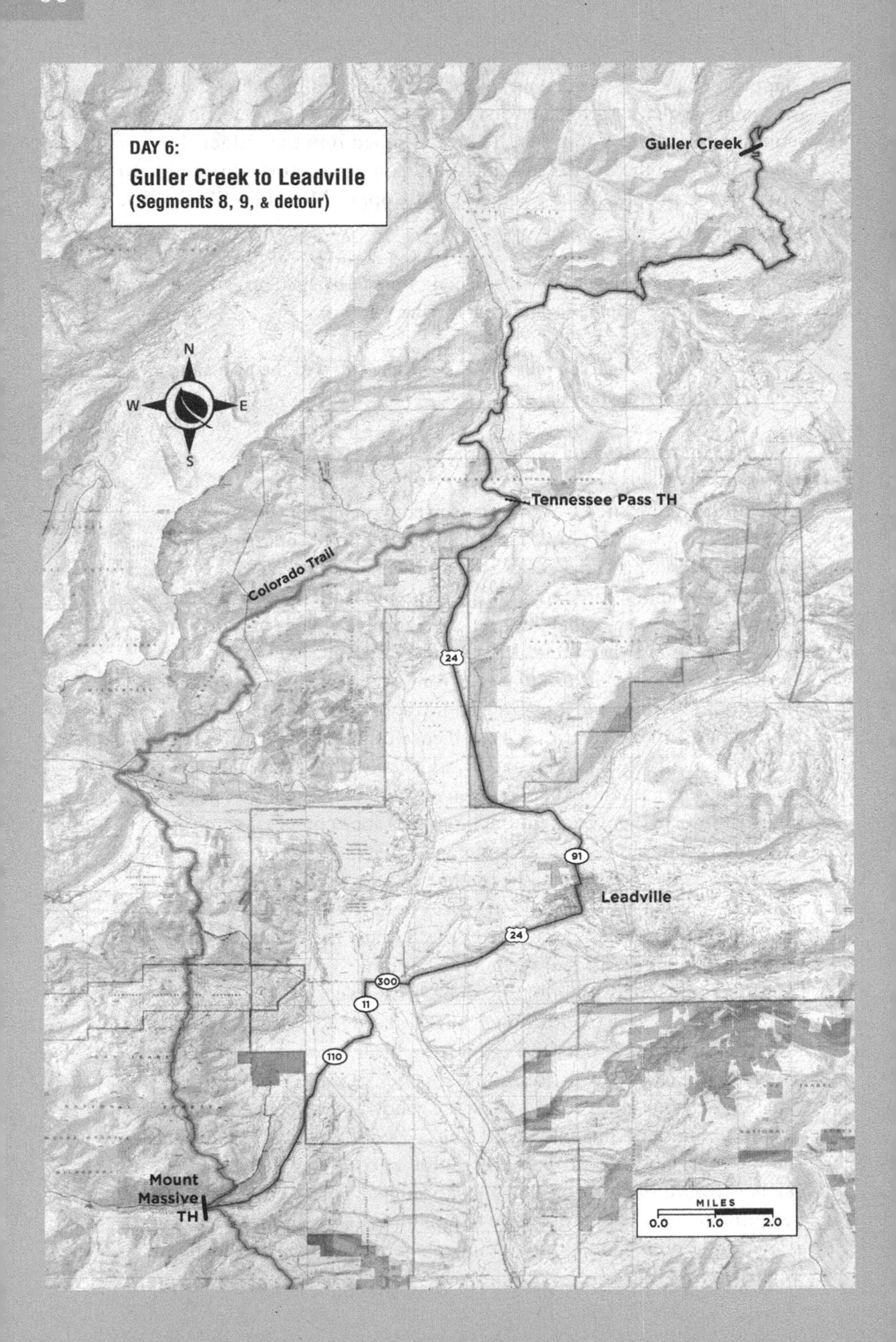
DAY 6:
Guller Creek to Leadville
(Segments 8, 9, & detour)
Guller Creek
N
W
E
S
Tennessee Pass TH
Colorado Trail
24
91
Leadville
24
300
11
110
Mount
Massive
TH
MILES
0.0
1.0
2.0

DAY 6 GULLER CREEK TO LEADVILLE SEGMENTS 8, 9, & DETOUR

SEGMENT 8 = 20.2 miles
SEGMENT 9 = 2.5
HOLY CROSS/MT. MASSIVE DETOUR = 10

TOTAL = 32.7 miles
VERTICAL = 3,870 + 150 + 405 = 4,425 feet

FUN FACTOR: 5
Kokomo and Searle passes, plus a raucous downhill into historic Camp Hale? Yes, please.

SUFFERFEST FACTOR: 3.5
Some extended climbing and rock fields. What else is new?

PUCKER FACTOR: 2.5
Could be higher if you take speed-related chances on the long downhill into Camp Hale.

BEAUTY FACTOR: 4.5
Kokomo and Searle are quite lovely, and Camp Hale is super neat. And probably haunted.

SUFFER QUOTIENT: 1,540

In the morning you'll be ready and raring to go. Yesterday's adventures—and real food—will have undoubtedly boosted your confidence and energy levels. Which is good, since you'll start the day climbing for a long stretch. Overall, the grind isn't too bad—mostly rideable, smooth singletrack in and out of forest, crossing Guller Creek several times, sometimes on cool little bridges, sometimes just trucking through the flow. Be sure to stock up on water here.

Yes, it's mostly rideable even with a fully-loaded bike, but there will be pitches that probably aren't worth it if you're planning on getting to Leadville. Overall, it's a pretty big day—lots of climbing, downhills, and time spent above 10,500 feet. But it's quite picturesque, and relatively remote. You're in it now. The Front Range and ski areas of Summit County are now gone. The last pitch to Searle Pass is classic alpine tundra—open views, few trees, a thin ribbon of singletrack marked by rock gardens, some rideable, some ankle-breakers. You'll settle into a routine that will become very familiar as the days accrue:

ABOVE My very sweet campground by Guller Creek.

ride, hike, suck wind, eat, drink. Repeat.

One new twist is all the day-riders cruising by on unburdened rigs. You may feel the temptation to try and keep up, and if you're a beast, you probably can. Keep in mind however, that you're the turtle, not the hare. Slow and steady wins the race. Especially when you're carrying your entire living situation, as turtles do—bedroom, kitchen, wardrobe, medicine cabinet, bike repair shop, and food pantry. That said, a little jolt of competitive juice never hurts. And it's kind of nice to see and chat with other riders, since encounters with fellow bikers will, in general, be few and far between on the Colorado Trail.

The apex of Searle Pass opens to gorgeous views in just about every direction—snowy peaks, long, meandering valleys, and if the weather is good, a big Colorado-blue sky. I suppose this is just one of the reasons why passes are good stopping points; they provide the opportunity to look back and reflect on what you've accomplished and where you've come from, and to feel good about all the hard work you put in. The metaphor here is obvious, and probably one of the reasons why you're out here: to step away from the endless hustle of life, take a deep breath, and look around. To gain some perspective.

There's this too: the chance to consider and plan for the trail that lies ahead.

Searle Pass is exactly this kind of retrospective threshold. And when you're done with nostalgic reveries, gird your loins and take a gander at what's in front of you. Dirt, mud, sweat, rock, and sky; sore ass, hands, feet, quads. More climbing, more tech, more beauty, more weather. Majestic views back toward the Tenmile Range and Janet's Cabin, nestled in the valley next to the one you've just climbed. Ahead, the run to Kokomo Pass and the Arkansas Valley basin, with several large mining operations and a large, glassy reservoir. You may be in the wild, but signs of humanity—and industry—still linger.

Day-bikers, should you meet up with any, will lend a party atmosphere—a nice contrast to some of the solitude one can experience (suffer from?) on this journey. At the top of the pass, I met up with a big happy group who took a photo for me and laughed at the obscene weight of my bike when one of the dudes struggled to pick it up. I envied their tiny packs and light rigs, but hey, I wasn't there for that. I was there to ~~suffer~~ *have a profound experience.*

The trail between Searle and Kokomo passes is what mountain biking at high altitude is meant to be—treeless, flowy, rugged, with some stream crossings and hike-a-bike. When I rode it, there were

ABOVE Kokomo Pass and my trusty steed.

ABOVE There's ample water to be found on this segment.

fields of snow and lots of puddles. And mud. In early August. By most accounts it hadn't been a particularly snowy winter. Be ready to leopard-spot your clothes, face, and gear when you hit the muck.

Searle Pass itself is an occasion for pure joy and sincere self-back-patting. You're at 12,027 feet, and what awaits is a blazing downhill to historic Camp Hale at 9,200 feet, where the 10th Mountain Division trained for winter warfare in WWII. If you're doing the math, yes, this means about 2,800 feet of downhill in six miles. A great time to rest those weary legs, but pay attention! You never know what's around the next corner—a downed tree, a hiker in the middle of the trail taking pictures of bees and flowers, a moose. If you have full-suspension rig: congratulations for slogging that extra apparatus with you. Here's where you get to fully appreciate it.

Ever since I moved to Colorado in 1997 and learned about Camp Hale, I'd wanted to visit. In many ways it's the birthplace of modern Colorado skiing: several of the 10th Mountain Division soldiers came back to Colorado after the war and founded major ski areas, including Vail, Beaver Creek, Keystone, and Winter Park. The camp itself sits in a large valley in the middle of nowhere. Besides a parking lot and a large placard, the only significant remnant of the camp you'll find is a long strip of concrete bunkers and signs encouraging folks to stay on the trail, since there may be unexploded ordinance still lying around.

(Man, I just love Colorado. Where else could this be a thing?) The bunkers themselves are not welcoming; they're stark, square, small, and windowless. There's plentiful water nearby, so stock up and hang out for a bit, imagining what it was like to be a solider training here, in the middle of winter, prepping to fight Nazis in the Italian Alps on super-long wood skis, wearing white snowsuits.

You've got about seven miles before reaching Tennessee Pass. The trail here is smooth singletrack, gently climbing about 1,400 feet before reaching its apex, so it's rideable, though all the climbing you did earlier will have taxed your legs a bit. Which is to say: if you're like me, it'll be slow but not terrible. Eventually the CT crosses Highway 24, which connects Minturn with Leadville. If you want, you can roadie it from here to Leadville if you are low on supplies or have a mechanical issue. The road probably isn't much easier—or faster—than the trail, which runs along a wide, flat valley, meandering in and out of trees before it hops onto an old railroad bed. The remnant climbs gently, is mostly straight, and there's not much to look at. Lots of sitting and spinning, kind of boring. There might be some saddle pain to keep you occupied. I remember a deep, glorious ache as I rode. It got so bad I had to stop and stand every few minutes to alleviate the agony. Eventually you'll pass a few old coke ovens, remnants of the busy rail lines that used to run through here.

If Leadville is your destination, keep pedaling! You've still got about 14 miles to this epic day, and keep in mind the rewards that await

ABOVE A Camp Hale bunker. It's not the coziest place, to be honest.

ABOVE More remnants of a thriving railroad and mining culture—a pair of coke ovens near Tennessee Pass.

you in Leadville: an actual bed and hot shower; hot food and cold beer; all the Snickers bars you could want.

The Tennessee Pass trailhead leaves you with a final decision for the day: again, you could roadie it into Leadville, or take a little bit of trail (about three miles) until you reach the start of the Holy Cross/Mr. Massive Detour. Either way, you'll spend some time on Highway 24. I recommend staying on the trail.

Once you get to Leadville—congrats! You've made it to a mountain town that's remade itself from a mining operation at 10,151 feet above sea level into an endurance athlete's paradise, famous for the Leadville 100 mountain-bike and trail-running races. It's a funky, fun little place, so relax for a bit and enjoy. If you do plan to stay the night, you might want to check ahead to make sure there's not one of those aforementioned races going on. Otherwise, every bed in town might be booked and the streets will be full of lithe, smooth-legged athletes.

Like you, maybe?

If you're going for the true rustic experience and want to camp, ride out of Leadville along the detour to the Mount Massive trailhead. Campsites can be found there, along with water in the flow of Halfmoon Creek, as well as additional camping about 1.5 miles in by Box Creek and Mill Creek. If, when you get to Tennessee Pass, you're totally beat and decide to wait until morning before gliding into Leadville, you can pitch your tent at Wurts Ditch, about 2.5 miles past the Tennessee Pass trailhead.

ABOVE Leadville has several historic saloons where one can wet one's whistle.

ABOVE Mountain culture is quite fascinating.

GRUB IN LEADVILLE

Golden Burro Café and Lounge: Affordable, flavorful Mexican fare.
High Mountain Pies: A rider's dream—pizza, wings, subs, and ribs.
Silver Dollar Saloon: Historic! Traditional pub fare.
City on a Hill Coffee: Coffee, and a tasty menu, too.

BIKE SHOPS

Cycles of Life: Best bike-shop name ever.
A full-service shop, with the requisite
laid-back atmosphere.
www.colbikes.com

PLACES TO STAY

There are lots of choices, from high-end to super-cheap.
Here are just a few:

Inn of the Clouds Hostel & Inn: cheap, with private
or shared rooms.
500 E 7th St, Leadville, CO 80461
(719) 486-9334
stayinntheclouds.com

Columbine Inn and Suites: basic motel stuff.
2019 N Poplar St, Leadville, CO 80461
800-954-1110
columbineinn.com

The Majestic: quaint and colorful,
with lots of character.
120 W 4th St, Leadville, CO 80461
(719) 427-9692
staymajestic.com

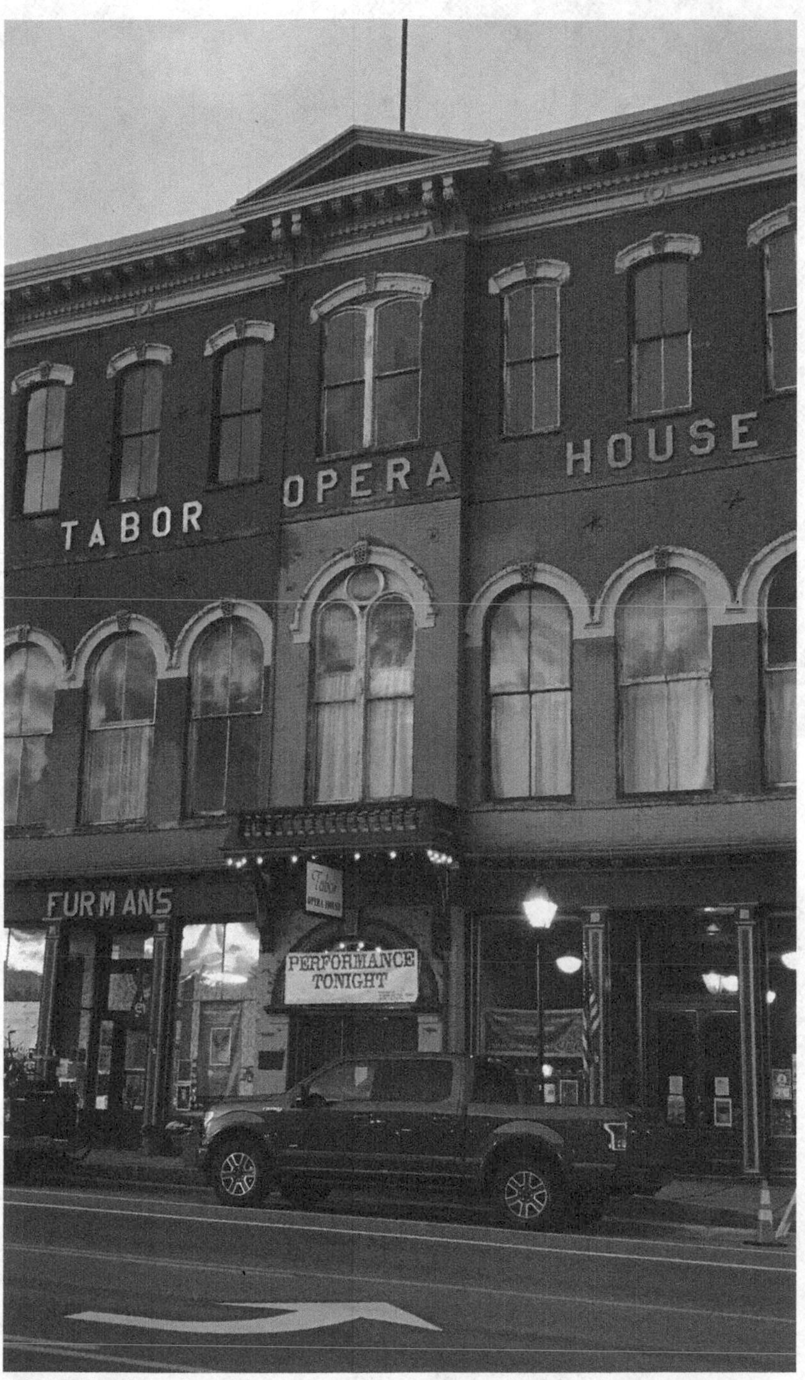

ABOVE The Tabor Opera House.

4 JC AND THE SPANIARDS

The last time I saw JC, I was on the lower stretches of Mount Elbert, the tallest peak in Colorado. I'd first met him on my initial day of riding, coming down toward the end of Segment 1 and the Platte River, flying toward him as he navigated a switchback on foot. He wore big hiking boots, white sweat socks, a windbreaker, and had a big, square handlebar bag. He was eager to chat me up, and I stopped to hear his story—one of the pleasures and welcome surprises of the Colorado Trail: who are you, where are you from, and why the heck are you out here?

JC was originally from North Carolina and had a sweet lilting accent and a big smile. He was enjoying himself immensely, and was thinking of riding just a few segments of the CT, with his wife running support in their car. Every day around suppertime, they met up and JC would be whisked off the CT to a nice dinner and hotel/motel bed. So far, so good. She'd dropped him off and planned to meet him at Little Scraggy trailhead. "It's hard going," he said, "but I think I'm doing pretty well for a 60-year old, don't you think?" I totally concurred.

Over the course of the next six days, I'd run into JC at various points: later that first day in the blazing heat of Segment 2; near Copper Mountain; just past Camp Hale; and on the way up the side of Mount Elbert. Eventually I found great comfort and camaraderie in the mere sight of him, chugging along on his old burgundy Specialized hardtail.

On the slopes of Searle Pass, JC caught me (my competitive juices were just a tiny bit less eager to see him, because he was riding with few encumbrances and was able to go pretty fast, considering) on the

LEFT Towards Foose Creek.
ABOVE Marshall Pass sign.

ABOVE Me at the top of Searle Pass. Taken by a new biker friend, JC.

long uphill. He'd hooked onto the back of two Spaniards who were riding the CT together. They were fully loaded like me, and were very nice, if quiet. We constituted a modest peloton up to the top of the pass, where we hung out for a while, trading stories and advice and newly acquired wisdom on bikepacking the CT. Eventually, the Spaniards and I dropped JC between Searle and Kokomo, and then I cruised past the Spaniards—both riding hardtails—on the crazy descent into Camp Hale. They promptly caught me there as I had lunch, and then, a few hours later, near Highway 24, JC caught me as I was replenishing my water supply. It's funny how you ride your own ride and spend lots of time in solitude, but then end up playing leap-frog with your fellow riders, seeing them every few hours. Back and forth we went, them ahead, then me ahead, then them, then JC.

I met up with the Spaniards at a coffee shop in Leadville the following morning, after we'd all spent the night in actual beds. I assume JC did, too, but we didn't run into him. We exchanged contact info and talked about the trail ahead. I was on my last day riding the CT, having planned to finish the next summer. The Spaniards were going all the way to Durango. A later email conversation confirmed they'd made it, and their intel on the trail ahead proved to be very helpful. They also recounted, with some exasperation, that JC followed them all the way, and one night when his wife didn't show (I'm guessing somewhere near Carson Saddle), they spent a stressful night in their tent with JC huddled outside, on the hard ground, wearing all the extra clothing they could offer him.

Like I said, the last time I saw JC was on the climb toward Mt. Elbert. I fully expected to meet up with him again, but never did. I wish I'd gotten his email address. I surely would have wanted to hear the story of how things went, and whether he made it all the way, and how he feels about such a task, years later. Instead, I have some fleeting memories and the genteel sound of his southern accent in my head. I'm not exaggerating when I say that I miss JC, though I hardly knew him.

Such is the nature of relationships on the CT. They are often unexpected, fleeting, and deeply memorable. There was the nurse I met as we both collected water from a stream on a bright, sunny morning. There were my dudes who convinced me to ride 285 instead of the Lost Creek detour. There was the guy riding the CT west to east, near Spring Creek Pass, his face covered in white paste, slathered with sunscreen. There was the very chill guy, also riding west to east, a wire basket attached to the front of his bike like he was just out to get some groceries. He'd warned me about the climb at the end of Fooses Creek, which he'd just ridden down. It's stupid steep, he'd said.

All these people are part of my journey. They are brothers and sisters in suffering, I suppose, which gives them, even in their stranger-ness, an intimacy that won't soon be forgotten. Which is one of the wonders of the Colorado Trail, I guess. And one of the paradoxes, too.

ABOVE Self-portrait at the CT high point. Don't I look like I'm having a great time?

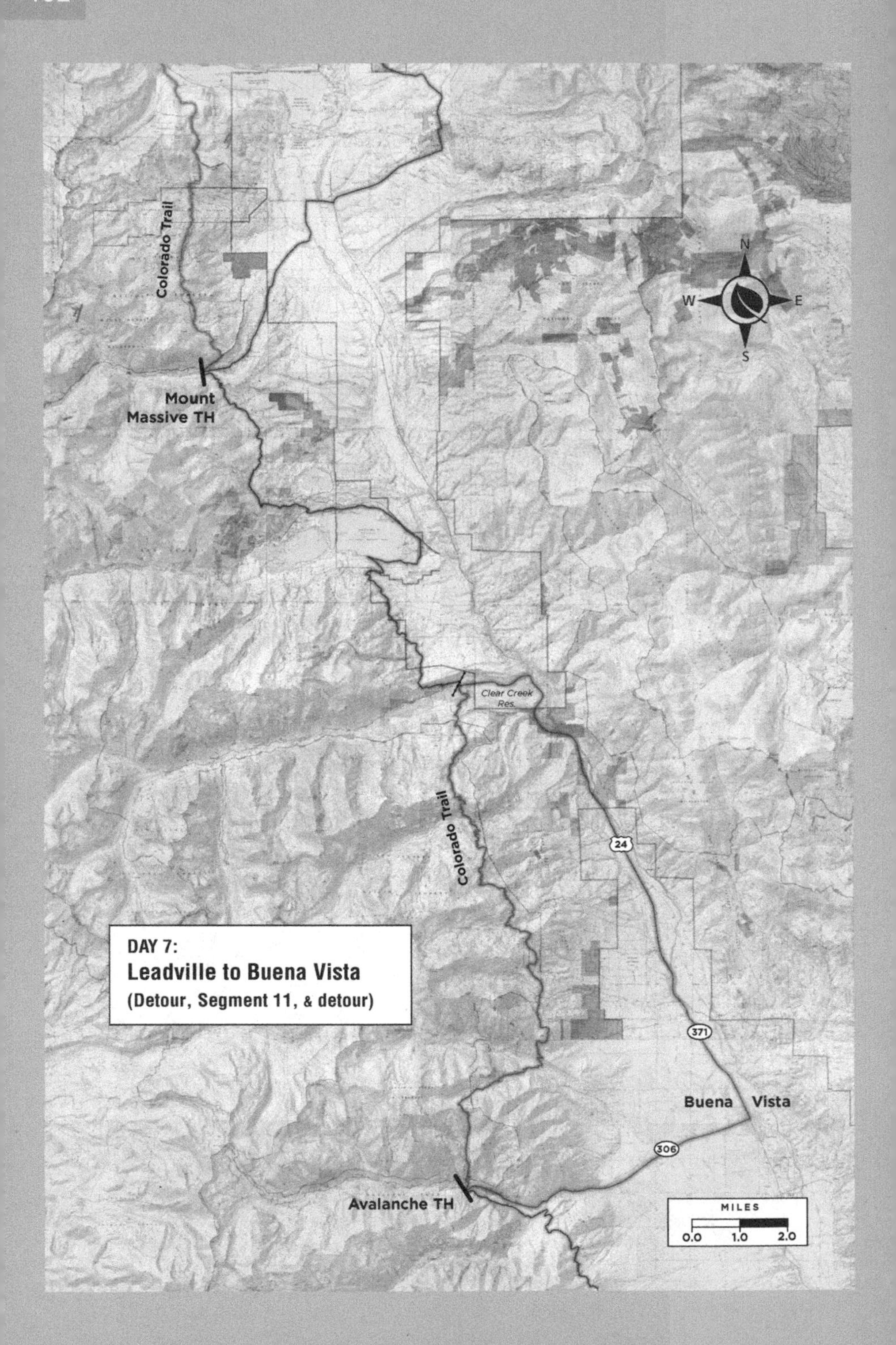
Colorado Trail
Mount
Massive TH
N
W
E
S
Clear Creek
Res.
Colorado Trail
24
DAY 7:
Leadville to Buena Vista
(Detour, Segment 11, & detour)
371
Buena Vista
306
Avalanche TH
MILES
0.0
1.0
2.0

DAY 7 LEADVILLE TO BUENA VISTA DETOUR, SEGMENT 11, & DETOUR

MT. MASSIVE DETOUR (LEADVILLE) TO START OF SEGMENT 11 = 11 miles
SEGMENT 11 = 21.5 miles
END OF SEGMENT 11 TO BUENA VISTA = 19 miles
TOTAL = 51.5 miles
VERTICAL = 506 + 2,910 + 188 = 3,604

FUN FACTOR: 3.5
Mount Massive is pretty awesome—especially the descent to Twin Lakes and the ride along the Arkansas River on the Collegiate Peaks Detour, not to mention some good riding in between.

SUFFERFEST FACTOR: 3.5
It will be a long day.

PUCKER FACTOR: 2.5
Some exposure on the downhill from Mt. Massive, but otherwise nothing to cry about.

BEAUTY FACTOR: 4.0
It's all just so majestic—and interesting, too.

SUFFER QUOTIENT: 684

ABOVE Mount Elbert is home to some impressive aspen forests.

The trail here enters a new landscape—a grand valley bordered by massive mountains—the Collegiate Peaks and three of the highest mountains in Colorado: Mount Elbert, Mount Massive, and Mount Harvard.

Did I mention that it will most likely be pretty hot? This is the Arkansas River valley, affectionately known as Colorado's Banana Belt, which is to say it's often blazing warm in the summer, and stays fairly warm in the winter, too. Except for Leadville. It can be wicked cold there any day, any time.

Today's adventure is book-ended by road rides, which are a nice break from all the singletrack. You can zone out and pedal at a decent speed. It's also your last opportunity to enjoy the trappings of civilization; once you eventually leave the Arkansas Valley you'll be in the most remote part of the Trail. There won't be much of anything except rugged solitude until you get to Silverton, about 100 miles away.

As for dirt, there's some awesome riding, a fair bit of climbing, and dense forest that skirts along Mount Elbert, where there will most likely be lots of happy and friendly day-hikers interested in your exotic bike and trappings. They'll undoubtedly want to hear all about your travails. The crowds thin out a bit after you pass the trail junction that leads to the peak of Mount Elbert, where there's also a parking lot. I'd bet the drive up is slow and a bit of a slog.

Your reward for this climb is a screaming downhill through aspen forest to Twin Lakes. This is the first of a couple of descents on the south side of ridges, so much so they'll begin to blend together in your mind, and you might ask yourself, *haven't I ridden this before*?

Once the downhill has been shredded and you're at the edge of Twin Lakes, if you're beat and done for the day, go right on the highway to the famous Twin Lakes general store; check ahead to make sure it's open. There's camping available up the road from the store.

If you're forging on, you'll curl around Twin Lakes then crunch back onto singletrack where you'll eventually reach the turnoff for the Collegiate West section of the CT. This is not for you, gentle rider, so make a sharp left turn and begin climbing along a steep face up to a ridge that overlooks Twin Lakes. Cross over the ridge, and kiss Twin Lakes goodbye.

Here there are more aspens, lots of up and down, some riding under electric power lines, and lots of trail junctions, which heightens the possibility of getting lost, so pay close attention! There are also a few really welcoming meadows, and then another fun downhill to Silver Creek trailhead, where the Collegiate Peaks detour begins. Go left on the gravel road, then right at Highway 24 for a bit, which isn't too bad—nice shoulder, not too crazy traffic (in general), and then cross over the

ABOVE Do not go Collegiate West, young person. Bikes are not allowed.

highway for a fun, fast, dirt road that passes through a series of really cool old railroad tunnels on the way to Buena Vista, and beer, and food, and maybe a bed with sheets and multiple puffy pillows.

You can stay in Buena Vista if you're a prima donna like me, or ride through town along Main Street and then turn west to finish the detour. There are a couple of campgrounds nearby. It adds about 10 miles, but it's mostly flat (okay, it's a gradual climb), and the ride is very peaceful.

GRUB IN BUENA VISTA

Brown Dog Coffee Company: Good breakfast eats, great coffee, really nice people.
Eddyline Brewery and Taproom: Good beer, good food.
The Jailhouse Craft Beer Bar: A really cool place—an actual historical jailhouse.

BIKE SHOPS

Black Burro Bikes
801 Front Loop, Unit 1A
Buena Vista, CO 81211
719-966-5045 | blackburrobikes.com

Buena Vista Bike Company
310 E Main St.
Buena Vista, CO 81211
(719) 966-5075 | www.bvbikeco.com

PLACES TO STAY

Mt. Princeton Hot Springs Resort
Why not stay in style and soak those weary muscles? Can be a little pricey.
15870 County Road 162
Nathrop, CO 81236
888-395-7799

Best Western Vista Inn
Nothing too fancy, but it'll do.
#733 U.S. Hwy 24 North
Buena Vista, CO 81211
719-395-8009

GENERAL INFO: buenavistacolorado.org

ABOVE Time to climb. And descend. And climb some more. With a fully loaded bike.

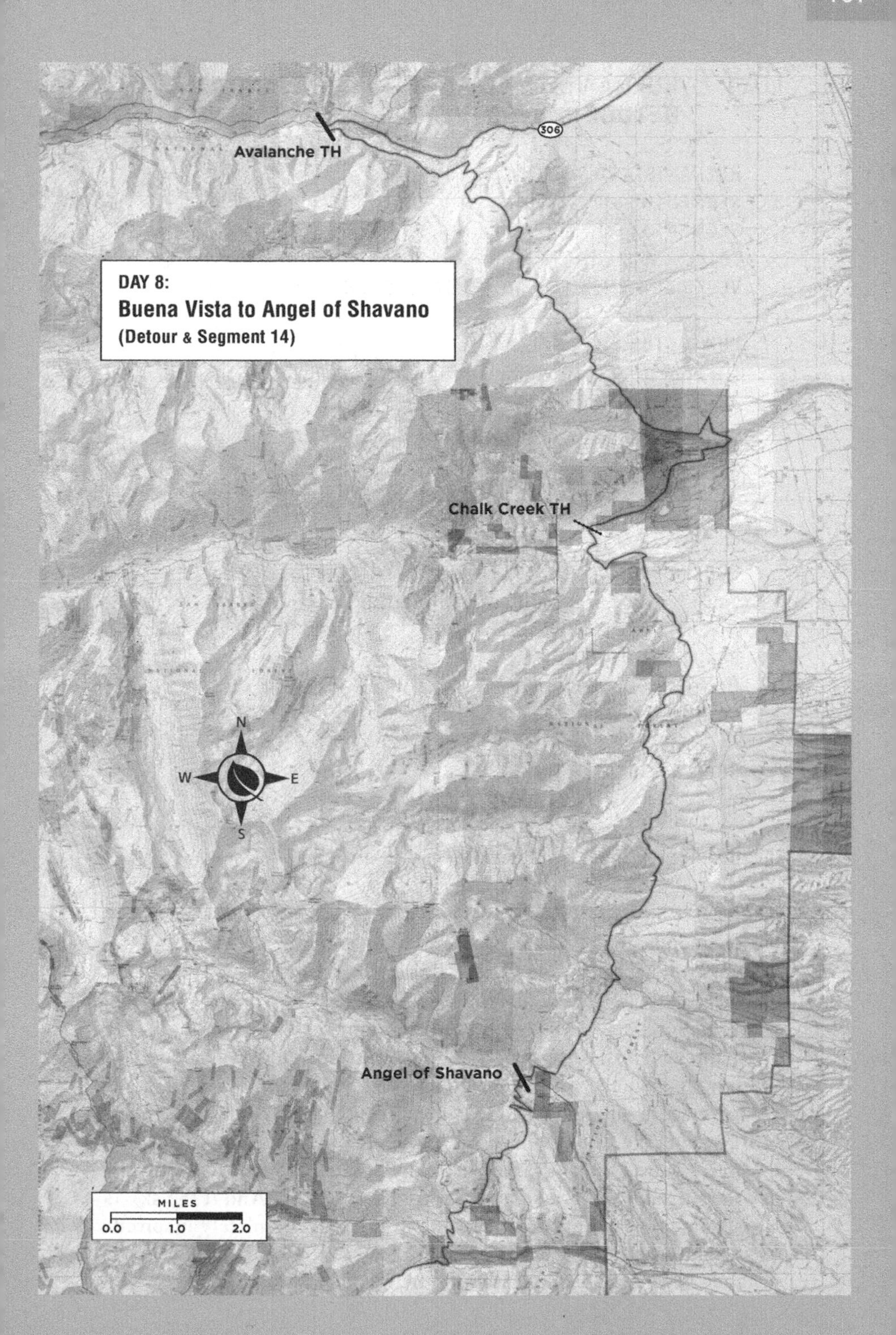
Avalanche TH
306
DAY 8:
Buena Vista to Angel of Shavano
(Detour & Segment 14)
Chalk Creek TH
N
W
E
S
Angel of Shavano
MILES
0.0
1.0
2.0

DAY 8 BUENA VISTA TO ANGEL OF SHAVANO DETOUR & SEGMENT 14

BUENA VISTA TO SEGMENT 13 = 10 miles
SEGMENT 13 = 16.1 miles
SEGMENT 14 = 12.7
TOTAL = 38.8 miles
VERTICAL = 1,452 + 1,596 + 2,510 = 5,558

FUN FACTOR: 2.5
It's honestly not all that exciting until you get close to Angel of Shavano.

SUFFERFEST FACTOR: 3
The main things are the many climbs and the possibility of stifling heat.

PUCKER FACTOR: 1.5
Nothing very scary, unless you're afraid of cows.

BEAUTY FACTOR: 3
Pretty forests and good views of Buena Vista and the Chalk Cliffs.

SUFFER QUOTIENT: 1,277

Not counting the roadie detour back to the CT, you'll be spending the day dipping in and out of many mountainside valleys, mostly in secluded forest, with the occasional open meadow, ridgeline, or roadway. If this ride were a day trip it'd be great—all mostly rideable, lots of smooth singletrack, a good mix of up and down, bucolic pastures full of cattle, pine forests—but with a fully-laden bike, you may get a little demoralized. And by fully laden I mean totally stuffed with supplies, since you have several long, hungry days looming.

I enjoyed most of this section but toward the end I was ready to unfurl and wave the white flag. I'd had enough. One thing to be proud of, however, is that you will log some decent miles. You'll mostly be rolling along the Collegiate peaks, which loom over Buena Vista and the entire valley. And yes, they are impressive; tall, rugged, a range of colors, from slate gray and white to a deep green. And if the sky is clear, domed by a haunting blue. One might feel completely inspired by such august beauty. In a way it's nice to see the mountains from a distance before you begin climbing them.

Some things to keep in mind: The first big climb of the day, after you finish the detour and reach the Avalanche Trailhead and the CT, is loose and steep, but not terribly long. You'll reach a promontory that has some great views, and what seems like the entire Arkansas valley. And then you'll roll, meandering along cattle pastures and nice, rolling terrain. There are many stream crossings, so water shouldn't be a problem. Overall, the day is one of those long, slow grinds where there isn't really a specific place that will tax you too much, but eventually all the pedaling will begin to fatigue your body. One fun thing: you'll eventually reach a wide dirt road that's a crazy-fast downhill, and then you've got some roadie riding before you roll up to Princeton Hot Springs, at which point you might be tempted to stop and soak for a bit. I wouldn't judge you if you did.

If you're continuing on, you'll roadie a short ways up to the Chalk Cliffs and begin another steep, loose, off-camber climb, which kind of sucks. When you eventually reach the top, again there's a nice view of the entire valley, and for a while after that the riding is awesome—fast, flowy, easy. Your brain might get a little blurry here, as the trail seems to repeat itself a bit.

The landscape gets even prettier as you get closer to your destination for the day—Angel of Shavano trailhead. There are some really beautiful aspen stands through here, and there will also be a fair amount of day hikers around, so watch those blind corners. You know how it goes: when you're rolling fast, not seeing anyone for hours, there will be a blind corner that you come to, and always—always!—someone's lying in wait to surprise you and make you lock your brakes and enter a death skid. That's just how it goes.

ABOVE The top of the Fooses Creek climb. When you get here, you'll feel like you've accomplished something.

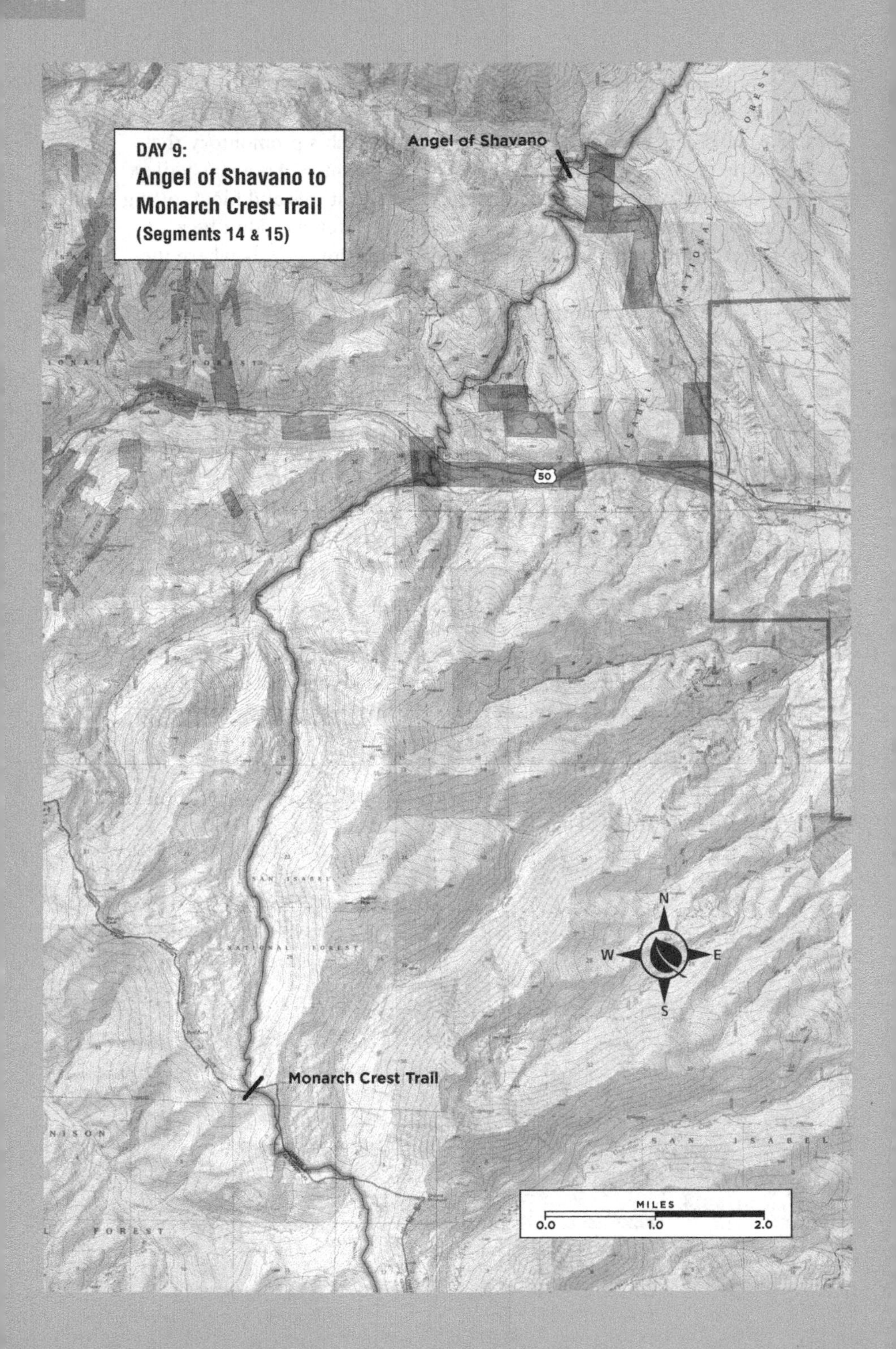
DAY 9:
Angel of Shavano to
Monarch Crest Trail
(Segments 14 & 15)
Angel of Shavano
Monarch Crest Trail
50
N
W
E
S
MILES
0.0
1.0
2.0

DAY 9 ANGEL OF SHAVANO TO MONARCH CREST TRAIL SEGMENTS 14 & 15

SEGMENT 14 = 5.3 miles
SEGMENT 15 = 10.3
TOTAL = 15.6
VERTICAL = 624 + 3,188 = 3,812

FUN FACTOR: 4
The link between Shavano and Highway 50 is pretty dang fun. The climb up Fooses is fun, too. And really, really hard.

SUFFERFEST FACTOR: 5
I'd give the final grind up to Fooses Creek a 5+.

PUCKER FACTOR: 2
The real scary thing is the steepness of today's climbing, and a few short, techy downhill stretches.

BEAUTY FACTOR: 3.5
4.5 once you reach the Continental Divide.

SUFFER QUOTIENT: 2,537

This might not seem like a big day, but it sure as hell is. The miles and vertical don't quite tell the whole story—it has the second highest Suffer Quotient of the entire trip. By day's end you'll be in a new landscape, having reached the Continental Divide yet again, topping out at 12,000 feet. You'll be leaving the Arkansas River valley behind for good, entering some pretty awesome high plains country. Ahead are some classic sections of the CT: Monarch Crest, the infamous Sargents Mesa, the serene yet endless La Garita detour, and CT high point just below Coney Summit. Once you cross Highway 50, you're on the most remote stretch of the trip; there's not much in the way of humanity until you get to Silverton.

If you've been lagging behind the plan laid out in this book, this may be a good day to play catch up and get some extra miles in. Or maybe you'll just want to survive.

You'll start the day much like the past few—in the forested lap of one of the Collegiate Peaks, riding up and over several ridges and stream crossings. There will be some short, challenging climbs, a few rollers, and two steep downhills, one at the Angel of Shavano trailhead, the second at the Route 50 crossover. Be careful on that last one—it's very loose and tricky in spots.

After crossing over Highway 50, the trail gradually transforms from a place of power lines and loud cars to lonely, serene high country. At first, the climb is long and mostly rideable on dirt road. Several miles in you'll reach a parking lot and a CT trailhead, and you'll cross over a bridge or two, and then you're back in the wild—and will be for the next few days. Your bike should be ready, you better have enough food, and you should be mentally geared up for some solitude because there ain't much around, nor is there an easy bailout in emergent situations, at least not until you reach Highway 149, which can take you down—and I mean *far* down—into Lake City. But that's far away.

Once you're back on the singletrack, the ride is absolutely resplendent—deep forest, tons of wildflowers, manageable riding. It's one of those magical sprite, fairy, and gnome forests, if you know what I mean. It stays like that until you get to rather long climb back up to the Continental Divide which goes on and on, until you reach a wall. The 800 yards or so and is one of the steepest sections of the CT. Inchworming is how it'll go, which, you'll remember, goes like this:

ABOVE More aspens, some nice riding.

1. **Stand next to bike—Ideally the left-hand side—with hands on handlebars;**

2. **Exhale and push bike ahead of you;**

3. **Clench front brake;**

4. **Step back up beside the bike, maybe whacking your shin against a pedal;**

5. **Breathe deeply in;**

6. **Repeat.**

You'll see the headwall long before you reach it. I suppose this is a case where seeing the challenge makes it less daunting. I mean, it's just a little snippet of trail, and the end—the razor-line of the ridge—is clearly in sight. There is no false summit.

Once you reach the top, take a moment to look back at what you've accomplished and say goodbye to the Arkansas Valley, the Collegiates, Buena Vista and the climb you've just crushed. Feel good about yourself, for you are a golden god!

Your reward is a flowy route along the ridge and sweet meadowlands until you come to a trail junction. About two miles in, there's the Green Creek shelter in a stand of trees just to the left of the intersection. Feel free to set up shop there for the night, though I found it a little gross and claustrophobic—it's three-sided, dark and dank, and has a dirt floor.

On my trip, I camped in an open meadow just before the junction, and when I woke in the morning, there were some visitors: three moose, wandering around the shelter. As the sun broke over the peaks, they casually foraged and munched as I, too, enjoyed my breakfast. All in all, it was a magical morning. And then I was on my way, on to the famous Monarch Crest Trail, where I soon met up with several gangs of day-bikers.

Monarch Crest is pure merriment. The vistas are wide open and the trail is fast, and mostly downhill. It'll all happen too fast, probably, because then you'll reach bottom and begin the slow work of climbing. What else is new?

5 THINGS FALL APART

Should every rider expect some sort of mechanical or gear-related challenge while on the CT? To put it simply: Hell yes.

In my research, pretty much every person who's ever embarked on the trail has encountered some sort of gear-related failure. A broken tent zipper. A slow-leaking tire that won't fully inflate. A pump that for some reason refuses to work. Rubbing brakes, which drives one batshit crazy as the miles—and squeaks—accumulate. A worn cable that's been crushed over time by a poorly hung handlebar bag (this happened to me), making the dropper post stay in the dropped position. (Not great for the quads.) A broken rear hub, rendering any pedaling useless, since the rear cassette spins without driving the tire forward, which means: time to walk. (This also happened to me.) Brake pads that wear down to nothing, compromising one's ability to stop. A broken chain, or spoke. A leaking suspension seal. And so on.

There are also human errors, which seem to fall in two categories: 1. Lack of attention; 2. Poor decision making. Both are often caused by exhaustion. Leaving tent stakes at the last campground, unrealized until you stop to set up camp the following day. Leaving an expensive camera on a log, two hours back. Is it worth the backtrack? Leaving your chamois out in the elements as a cold rain falls, all night. A shattered water bladder and phone after

LEFT Sure, enjoy life, but it can wear you down, obviously.
ABOVE Yet another grand view.

a crash, when you slid off trail at high speed because you were fried and not focusing on the trail ahead. Dropping your last energy bar on the ground because you tore the stupid packaging open with too much force (I've done that a million times). Leaving your toothbrush on a rock at a campsite at 12,000 feet (did that too).

Yes, bad things happen, and yes, bad things certainly happened to me. Or should I say: I did dumb things. The shattered hub was the worst by far, however, and not my fault. Thankfully this happened near Salida on Segment 14. I walked about six miles—which really, really sucked, by the way, just saying—to a road, then coasted down to Highway 50 where I was, and I know this sounds improbable, able to procure an Uber into town. The good folks at Absolute Bikes set me up with a new wheel and a new pair of bike shorts. They also tuned the bike for me. I love those people. They were awesome. (It cost me about $500, but what else could I do?)

Do I have any advice on how to prevent mechanical issues and mental failures? Not really. I mean, it happens. I suppose there are some things you can do to try and prevent such small disasters. But first, let's admit it: these are first-world problems, and we are incredibly fortunate and blessed to be able to put ourselves in these sorts of hard situations as a matter of enjoyment, not survival.

Second, as I've said earlier: test out your gear and make sure everything is ready to go. Check items for wear. Get the bike tuned up and looked over by an experienced mechanic—someone who knows that you're going to be out on the CT. But also ride it a few times before your journey. As good as a mechanic is, sometimes they "fix" something but don't exactly get it right. I've said it earlier, but it bears repeating: Bring basic repair tools—multi-tool, small patch kit for your tent and sleeping pad, extra tubes, a bit of chain and chain-breaker tool (if it's not on your multi-tool), extra brake pads and shoe cleats. Lube your chain. Check your tires and spokes for anything suspicious.

Third, try not to be careless. Before you're ready to leave camp, take a deep breath, clear your mind, and look around. Have you forgotten anything? Stay present and focus on what's around you. Try not to get too into your head. Be in the moment. Double-check straps, zippers, ties. Make decisions, and then rethink them. If you get to a fork in the trail and are unsure where you're supposed to go, stop and take a look at FarOut or the *CT Guidebook* and make sure. Look at a sign, then look at it again, making sure you're reading it correctly. Sometimes the way the CT signs and arrows point don't seem to make a lot of sense, and you can decide on one thing, which is the wrong thing. Backtracking is no fun.

I say all this assuming that you'll be alone; if you have a riding buddy or a gang of like-minded fools with you, that'll make life a lot easier. Oftentimes, one person will take the lead and be the focused, triple-checking cartographer/human compass/GPS system, and maybe another can serve as gear boss, and then maybe there's a bike boss, and so on. Roles may hop from person to person, and when you're not in the lead position you can totally zone out and be a space cadet, like I usually am. That'll take some of the pressure off.

Also, bring a credit card. You just might find yourself in a town buying replacements for all the things you carelessly dropped, used up, broke, or left somewhere, or you'll be at local bike shop getting repairs or replacement parts that you'd never imagined needing.

Someday, I'll get back to Segment 23 and Lost Creek, and I will find that toothbrush. I am not a litterbug.

ABOVE While getting my bike fixed in Salida, I was able to procure a new pair of shorts to help deal with some rawness in my undercarriage. They were very shiny.

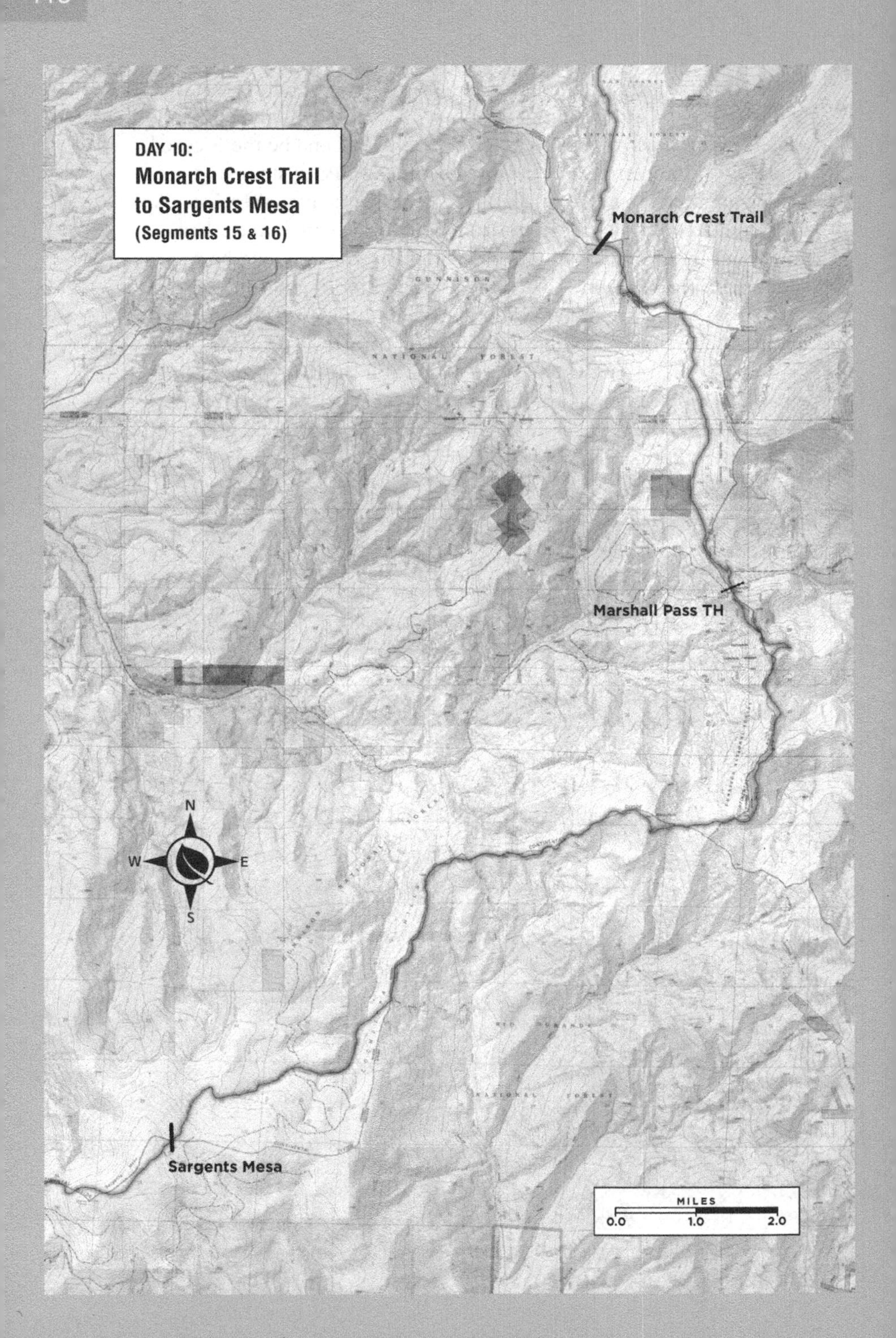
DAY 10:
Monarch Crest Trail
to Sargents Mesa
(Segments 15 & 16)
Monarch Crest Trail
GUNNISON
NATIONAL FOREST
Marshall Pass TH
N
W
E
S
RIO GRANDE
NATIONAL FOREST
Sargents Mesa
MILES
0.0
1.0
2.0

DAY 10 MONARCH CREST TRAIL TO SARGENTS MESA SEGMENTS 15 & 16

SEGMENT 15 = 9.0
SEGMENT 16 = 15.2
TOTAL = 24.2 miles
VERTICAL = 408 + 3,184 = 3,592

FUN FACTOR: 3.5
Can't beat a ride on Monarch Crest trail.

SUFFERFEST FACTOR: 3.5
It seems like it should be a simple day, but there's something going on here.

PUCKER FACTOR: 1
No steeps, no sketch, little to worry about. But if you're going to crash, it's probably here. That's just how it goes, am I right?

BEAUTY FACTOR: 3
Monarch is very purdy—rolling greens and forests and distant peaks purdy.

SUFFER QUOTIENT: 1,668

Remember one the great thrills of mountain biking? Namely, cruising fast and flowy on sweet, smooth trail, and actually staying on the bike for extended periods of time, not having to climb off and trudge onward with your feet on the ground, constantly lamenting how awkward bike shoes are to walk in, consistently mashing your shins against your pedals? Who can forget those moments of ease and bliss.

The opening stretch of today's ride continues on the Monarch Crest trail, which means that you'll be more rider, less hiker. Take it all in! Enjoy every freaking pedal stroke and downhill stretch, because, as you know, you may cover lots of miles in this fashion, but time spent in this mode is fleeting, and before you know it you'll be back to hike-a-bike, covering one tenth of the distance in the same amount of time.

If you get up relatively early, you'll be joined by lots of day riders on this section, as it's a popular shuttle-service ride. It's kind of fun to see if you can keep up; the good vibes of shiny happy mountain biking people will make it even more fun. Soon enough you'll reach the trailhead at Marshall Pass Road, and then, about four miles in, you'll leave Monarch Crest trail. Stay right, and then goodbye to decent

ABOVE On the way to infamous Sargents Mesa

biking. Begin saying things like, "But it shouldn't be this lousy! The *Guidebook* says so! Begin saying things like, "But it shouldn't be this lousy! The *Guidebook* says so! Be careful here—there are many trail junctions, and it can be easy to take a wrong turn.

This is where it gets real. Lots of up-and-down steeps, lots of very—and I mean VERY—loose sections. You'll enter a kind of a miasma, a dreamlike state. Ride, hike, crawl, ride, hike, crawl. Eat, drink. Cover the feet, yards, meters, and miles, slow but sure. As poet Theodore Roethke once wrote, "I wake to sleep, and take my waking slow. / I feel my fate in what I cannot fear. / I learn by going where I have to go."

Today's destination is Sargents Mesa, the infamous stretch that is shared with motocross bikes, horses, and all manner of trail-destroying animals and machines.

I myself thought this post-Monarch section was Sargents Mesa, mostly because it totally stunk. The loose, rocky, punishing, meanly laid out climbs—and by "climbs" I mean a ribbon of baby-head boulders going straight up the fall line—totally sucked.

Have I said this before? The Colorado Trail is a very rugged hiking trail that allows bikes.

When I finally got to the segment's end and set up camp, I was a little surprised and maybe even a tiny bit deflated when I looked at the *Guidebook* and saw that the well-documented horrors of Sargents Mesa still lay before me. And so it begins, or continues, maybe: the oft-held sensation that you've been tricked, or lied to, or haven't been told the honest truth. Like when you look at the elevation chart's squiggly line and you think, *heck, that's not so bad*, but somehow the scale doesn't register, and what you experience is ten times worse than it seems like it should be. You might find yourself shouting out loud in the woods, things like, "But it shouldn't be this lousy! The *Guidebook* says so!" And so forth.

To put it in the form of an equation: Gravity + loose, rocky trail + what looks like modest elevation gain = a dirty, terrible falsehood. If only you knew the actual truth, you might not have done this stupid ride after all.

I allowed such thoughts to enter my mind many, many times. And yet there was nothing I could do about it. I was out there, far away from everything.

Back to the day's ride. Eventually the world around you levels off into a high mesa with mountains emerging across vast distances. The trail settles into a gently climbing double-track, all rideable. There will most likely be cows, and copses of gray-red lodgepole pine forests, dead from pine beetle infestation. And maybe some skeletal parts, too. I found a fair bit of what I believe were the bones of a cow or two, smooth and bleached white. All the dead trees, not unlike the bones, are a little sad, but already there are signs that the forest—mostly aspen and ponderosa pine—are coming back.

When you reach the end of the segment, you'll feel very alone. It's not a bad feeling, though some have reported feeling creeped out, feeling that the area is haunted. If you have time, I highly recommend checking out Soldierstone, a little ways back from the segment's end

ABOVE This might seem like Sargents Mesa, but you're not there yet. (Yes, that's the trail.)

and off the trail. How it got there I can't really figure out. Might have been dropped in by helicopter. It'll be a solemn, quiet moment, and you may wonder at the human spirit, and how we should never forget such events like the Vietnam War, nor should we forget the small struggles we all endure—from the losses of loved ones, losses of comfort and happiness, and how we are, literally always on a trail, forging onward with our own private journeys, and how this trip is both a lesson and a metaphor: all one can do is keep going on, one pedal stroke, one step, at a time.

ABOVE Soldierstone.

ABOVE There's something deeply poignant about this monument, sitting out in the wilderness.

More on Soldierstone: I had an older second cousin that went to Vietnam, and though I learned little of his experience, when he returned I could tell he was profoundly changed. I was just a kid at the time, but there seemed to be something laconic and sad about him, and he drifted from job to job, living with my great aunt for a while, growing his hair long. I remember he loved to play guitar and sing, and at a few family parties he'd play for us, his eyes closed, his mind far away, lost in the music. And on the 4th of July, at family celebrations, he liked to blow up my old model airplanes with M-80s, but that's another story.

After I set up camp and had some dinner, I walked back down the trail, then turned off and bushwacked to Soldierstone, which I could just barely see in the distance. When I got there, I couldn't help but think about my cousin. I remembered one of the best books I've ever read, a memoir cloaked in the garment of a novel, *The Things They Carried*, and the heartbreak and horror the author, Tim O'Brien, himself a Vietnam vet, described. How the war haunted an entire generation, and how this monument, like the memorial in DC, isn't a statue of people, but an abstraction, as if direct representation would be foolish.

Out in the literal middle of nowhere, Soldierstone began as a dream of Vietnam vet Stuart Allan Beckley, who worked with stonemason Mike Donelson to carry out his vision. Beckley wanted to do something because, as Donelson once said in an interview, "I always had the feeling that he had remorse—some things that were eating in his gut that I know had to have happened in Vietnam with his men. There's a lot of stuff, because he was a lieutenant colonel, that was revealed on a need-to-know basis."

The memorial was completed in 1995, a few months before Beckley passed away. His vision of having no obvious signage or pathway leading to the memorial continues to be honored.

I'm not saying that riding the CT is anything like going off to war—it's not even close—but something about this passage from *The Things They Carried* resonates:

> After a firefight, there is always the immense pleasure of aliveness. The trees are alive. The grass,

the soil—everything. All around you things are purely living, and you among them, and the aliveness makes you tremble. You feel an intense, out-of-the-skin awareness of your living self—your truest self, the human being you want to be and then become by the force of wanting it. In the midst of evil you want to be a good man. You want decency. You want justice and courtesy and human concord, things you never knew you wanted. There is a kind of largeness to it, a kind of godliness. Though it's odd, you're never more alive than when you're almost dead. You recognize what's valuable. Freshly, as if for the first time, you love what's best in yourself and in the world, all that might be lost. At the hour of dusk you sit at your foxhole and look out on a wide river turning pinkish red, and at the mountains beyond, and although in the morning you must cross the river and go into the mountains and do terrible things and maybe die, even so, you find yourself studying the fine colors on the river, you feel wonder and awe at the setting of the sun, and you are filled with a hard, aching love for how the world could be and always should be, but now is not.

ABOVE "Abandon hope all ye who enter here."

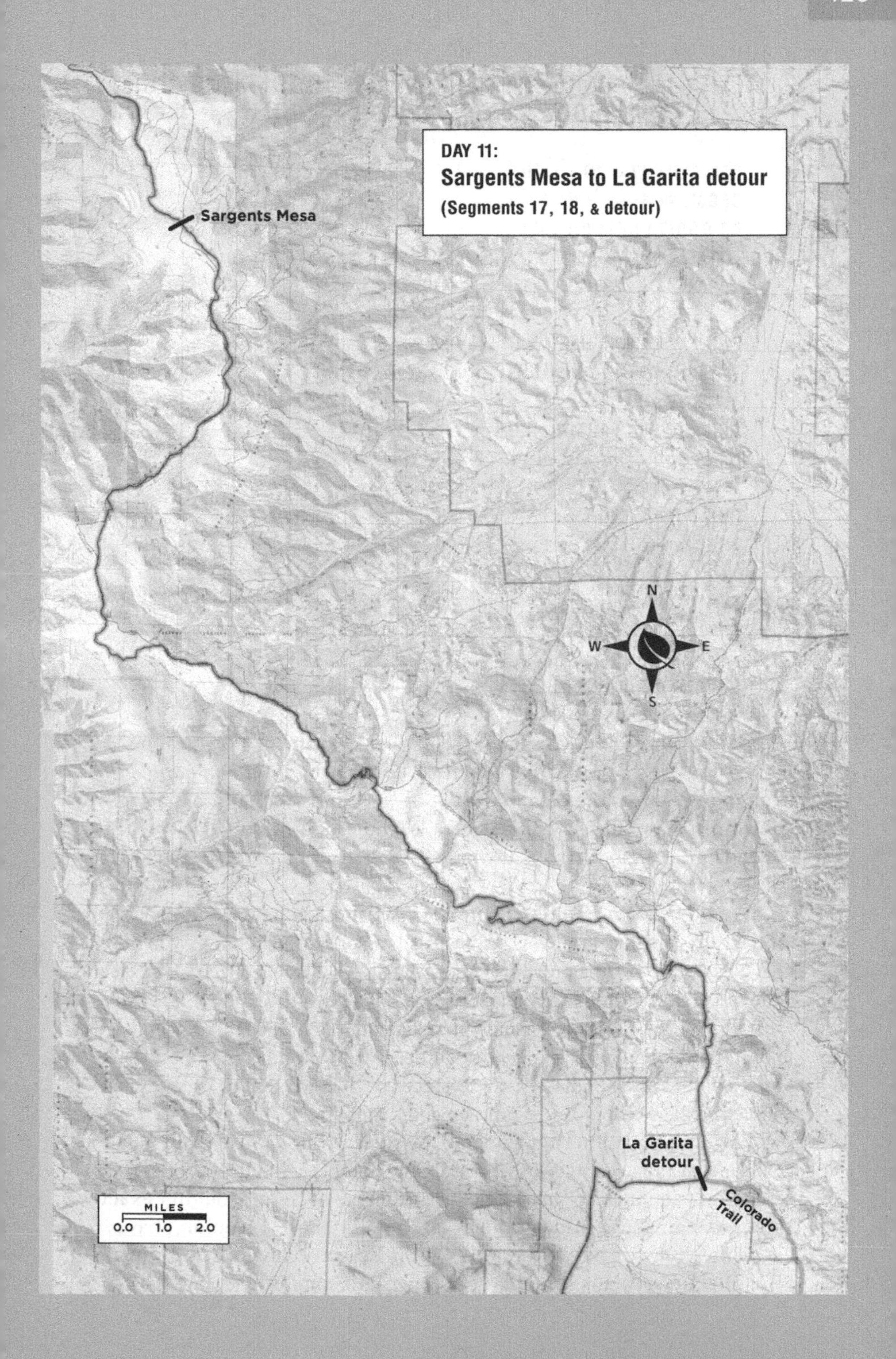
DAY 11:
Sargents Mesa to La Garita detour
(Segments 17, 18, & detour)
Sargents Mesa
N
W
E
S
La Garita
detour
Colorado
Trail
MILES
0.0
1.0
2.0

DAY 11 SARGENTS MESA TO LA GARITA DETOUR SEGMENTS 17, 18, & DETOUR

SEGMENT 17 = 20.4 miles
SEGMENT 18 = 13.8
LA GARITA DETOUR = 4.9
TOTAL = 39.1
VERTICAL = 2,810 + 1,259 = 4,069

FUN FACTOR: During Sargents Mesa: 0.0. After that, 4.0.
This place is a purgatory of lousiness.

SUFFERFEST FACTOR: 4.0
Not a ton of miles, but it's a long day.

PUCKER FACTOR: 1
Nothing to be afraid of.

BEAUTY FACTOR: 3.5
Sargents Mesa is not very nice. The rest is pretty great.

SUFFER QUOTIENT: 2,281

At first, when you embark on Sargents Mesa, Segment 17, you'll be thinking: *What's all the fuss about? This isn't so bad. I can handle this.* You might look at the data in the *Guidebook* and see that it's mostly downhill, and will feel emboldened. And these things will be true. For about a mile or so. Perhaps the only saving grace is that Sargents Mesa is not terribly long.

You'll be riding a little, hiking a lot. What might be frustrating is that, if the rocky mess of trail was only yards long at a stretch, and if you didn't have bags full of stuff on your bike, you might be psyched to try and clean a few sections. But it goes on and on and on. Tiny bits of smooth, rideable sections quickly deteriorate and you're back in the mess. If you want to be a total nerd and give every rock garden a try, you'll be hopping off and back on the saddle endlessly. The chances of twisting and/or breaking an ankle increase with every saddle-up and dismount.

At first, I tried to ride/navigate the rocky, rooty, loose, baby-head carpet that is Sargents Mesa, then I gave up and walked. For long stretches. So much so that I'd get to a rideable section, wouldn't exactly recognize it, and would continue walking. After all, I wouldn't have gone much faster, and surely wasn't going to save any energy riding. But of course, this is just me. A stronger, more ambitious, better-balanced rider might have a much easier time, and might ride 80% of this segment. Good luck with that.

I know this is a whole lot of negativity, so let me say something positive. What's the best thing about Sargent's Mesa?

It eventually ends.

The trail finally reaches a long, sort of rideable downhill, then spits you out onto a dirt road. Take a moment and pat yourself on the back: you've freaking made it! The next long stretch—which includes all of Segment 18—is super easy riding.

You'll ride this dirt road for a bit, and then you'll reach CO Highway 114. Eventually you'll cross the highway; make sure to keep your eyes open for the crossing, otherwise you'll needlessly have to climb back up the highway. I did that, and was not very happy about it.

Once you reach the other side, pop through the gate, and enjoy riding through a very green, lush, open valley, then up what seems like an old railroad bed to a saddle you'll cross over. Here's the one climb you might need to hike-a-bike, but while it's steep, it's also blissfully short. This is maybe the easiest segment of the entire CT.

If you are suffering, take comfort: ahead is where Apple, the famous trail angel, usually sets up camp. Think: snacks and cold soda. After Apple's camp, the La Garita detour begins. The next 60-plus miles will be on roads, and I have to say, it's a nice break after the ridiculousness of Sargents Mesa. You actually get to sit and pedal through a really lovely and very remote area of Colorado, dotted with old ranches, interesting landscapes and rock formations, and two hella-long but manageable climbs.

If you're done for the day, there's a great and often empty campground at the far end of Dome Lakes, about five miles into the detour. There's a pump for water, too. Sunset by the Lakes is a great way to close out the day.

ABOVE A few curious (non-skeleton) bovines at the beginning of the La Garita Detour.

6 TRAIL ANGELS AND OTHER FOLKS: THE PEOPLE YOU MEET ON THE COLORADO TRAIL

On my ride, there were three occasions when I needed help, when I was just about at my wit's end, when my body was telling me *nope* and my brain was pulling the emergency alarm, but no one was around to come to my aid.

And yet, at each one of those moments, a trail angel suddenly appeared, and saved my life.

I exaggerate only slightly. The first time I encountered a trail angel—actually, an entire camp full—I'd just exited Sargents Mesa. I was beat tired and mentally deflated by all the hike-a-bike. I was also running low on food, and still had at least three days before resupply in Silverton.

I'd just screamed down a long downhill, hit a dirt road, and there they were: Jan and Pooh, in an extensive camp set-up, with a porta-potty, a grill, several campers and pickup trucks, and more food than you'd find at a corner 7-11.

I could not believe my luck. Not only was I able to save one of my dehydrated dinners for later, I was able to load up with goodies—cookies, chips, apples, soda, and more. And they fed me—three hot-dogs, macaroni salad, brownies, Fritos. Not to mention the wonder of human-to-human conversation. Jan and Pooh and their gang—about five other lovely women, either retired or current schoolteachers—wanted to know who I was, how my ride was going, where I lived, what I did for a living, and why I'd decided to ride the Colorado Trail. They told me their

LEFT It can seem a little lonely out here, but trail angels will renew your faith in humanity.

stories, too—how they'd hiked the Colorado Trail the summer before, and how they'd decided that the next year they had to, absolutely had to, come out and spend a few weeks serving as angels.

And angels they were. I left with a full tummy, snacks packed into every cranny on my bike, and a renewed sense of humanity. Best of all, I felt nurtured, adored even, by these total strangers. They were all mother figures for a brief, shining moment, and I'll never forget them.

The second time I needed an angel I found someone, went up to them, and asked for help. ("Begged" might be a better descriptor.) It was a dark time. Toward the end of the La Garita detour, I'd been climbing for what seemed like days. It was blazing hot and dry, and the road was steep. I was a little freaked out because that morning I'd collected water from a deep, lazy stream, and then as I rode uphill, I realized that there were miles of cow pasture—and cow pies—that drained into said lazy stream. I'm sure it was psychosomatic, but my stomach began churning and I grew weak. I kept stressing about getting sick and maybe puking my guts out, and the anxiety itself made me think I *was* sick. I'd refilled my water soon after from a clear stream, but still felt parched and ill. And yet the detour—a dirt road climbing out of the Cebolla Creek drainage—continued on. I had no idea when it might end.

See below, Day 12, for more on that.

A trio of large pickup trucks were slowly making their way up the road. They passed me by, then stopped to chat for a bit. When I caught up, I stopped and stared at the group of people milling around. They stared back. I nodded toward a relatively empty bed in one of the trucks and said, "Could you possible give me a ride up to the top of this lousy road?"

One gentleman kindly said yes. And so I rode in the back, hanging onto my bike, three little kids staring at me through the rear window.

When we finally reached Highway 149, relief washed over me, even though I still had about nine miles to go before reaching the end of the detour. I probably could have made that climb, but man, I was so hot, thirsty, queasy, and tired. I really needed break.

Thank you to that nameless dude and his family, and their big old pickup.

The third trail angel saved my ass on Stony Pass Road, but more on that later.

One thing about angels: Like grace, they are a gift that appears out of nowhere, out of the ether, maybe, and their only desire is to make sure you're safe and all set with things you need, and then they send you on your way, asking for nothing in return. You will most likely never see them again, but you will spend the rest of your life singing their praises at odd, mundane moments, perhaps when you bite into a cold, crisp apple, or tear open a bag of Fritos.

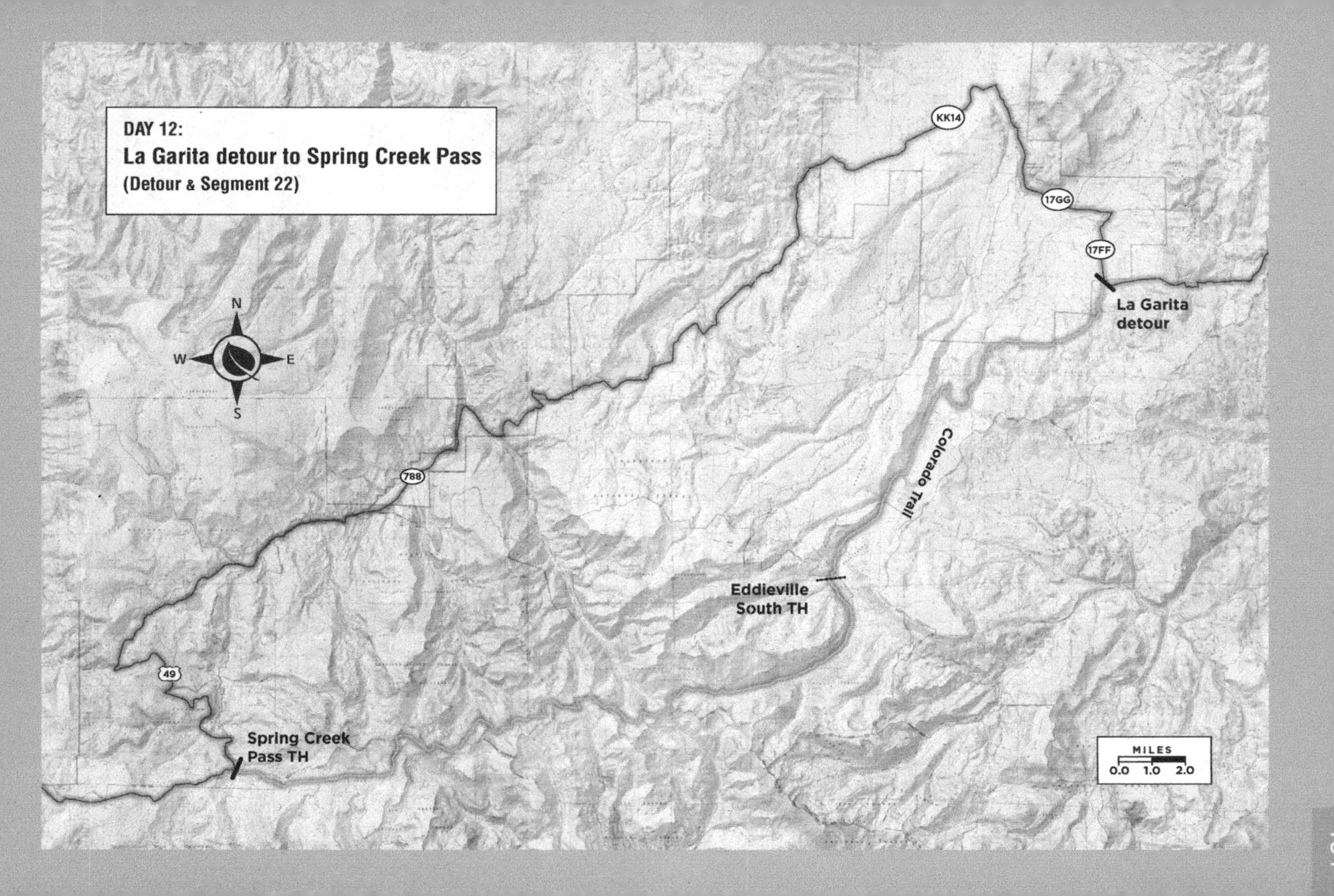
DAY 12:
La Garita detour to Spring Creek Pass
(Detour & Segment 22)
N
W
E
S
KK14
17GG
17FF
La Garita detour
788
Colorado Trail
Eddieville South TH
49
Spring Creek Pass TH
MILES
0.0 1.0 2.0

DAY 12 LA GARITA DETOUR TO SPRING CREEK PASS DETOUR & SEGMENT 22

LA GARITA DETOUR = 52 miles
SEGMENT 22 = 3.3
TOTAL = 55.3
VERTICAL = 5,241 + 324 = 5,565

FUN FACTOR: 4
It's kinda nice to be on the road and seeing all the pretty horses. And cows.

SUFFERFEST FACTOR: 5
Mileage and heat.

PUCKER FACTOR: 1
Mostly it's just empty roads.

BEAUTY FACTOR: 4
Not high mountains, but some very attractive cattle-ranch type landscapes.

SUFFER QUOTIENT: 2,039

ABOVE The journey continues.

A question: Are you in a gravel-rider mind-frame, and if not, can you get into one? Today is all road, all day long, with more than 5,500 feet of climbing. Lots of time in the saddle, lots of relaxed pedaling, lots of slow uphill grinding with no worries about rocks, roots, or switchbacks. Get up to speed, keep on rolling, and enjoy the scenery. Overall, it's some of the prettiest views you'll see—not high, rugged mountains, but rolling fields and pristine Colorado farm country. Make sure you have enough water, because while there are lots of water sources, you're going to drink a ton today. Most of the ride is under open sky, and most likely it'll be pretty hot. If you're like me and prefer to exert yourself in cool weather, I'm sorry. Get that sunscreen on and get ready to sweat. And don't even try filtering the water by the many cow pastures. It's nasty.

For most of the morning you'll roll along on dirt roads, past ranch land. About 16 miles in, you'll begin a long gradual climb up to San Luis Pass, followed by a blissfully long downhill. Eventually you'll enter a narrow valley along Cebolla Creek, and then a huge, super slog of a climb begins. Enjoy! The pain might not be intense, but it will be persistent. And let me just say, when I rode this section, it was supremely hot. I was also close to running out of water, stupidly, because I didn't fill my camelback all the way when I'd last stopped at the start of the climb.

All of which is to say: I was a mess. Sometimes you get into that zombie space where all you can focus on is the slow creep forward when you should stop and take care of your needs—food, water,

ABOVE Apple's Trail Angel Camp.

sunscreen, nagging butt pain, pebble in shoe. A bit of advice: take care of your needs. (Duh, right?) If you do that, then your ride might actually end up going a tiny bit faster, making up any time you've spent crouched over a stream getting H20, or sitting on a log and methodically pulverizing a Clif Bar between your tired teeth, or stretching, or adjusting a sock, or whatever.

Me, however, I didn't stop. Like a dope. As I said before, eventually I got so fried I ended up begging a guy in a huge pickup truck to give me a ride to the highway. I sat in the pickup bed and chilled for a while, which I enjoyed very much, even if I felt like a cheater. There are worse sins.

Once you reach Highway 149, if you really, desperately need to resupply or have a serious mechanical issue, you'll want to turn right and descend miles and miles (actually only about 10) into Lake City. It looks like a very a painful climb to get back on track, so I'd suggest doing that only if the situation is dire.

Go left on Highway 149 in order to continue the detour. Things smooth out a bit and there are a few downhills followed by a not-so-bad paved-road climb up to Spring Creek Pass. There's a parking lot at the trailhead, and the blissful fresh elixir of Spring Creek on the side of the highway. About a mile or two in on Segment 22 there's a large, flat meadow—a perfect camping spot.

Get your rest. The next two days are going to be epic. You're at 10,901 feet, and the trail all the way to Silverton stays well above that.

ABOVE Day 13, the trail takes you to the top of the world.

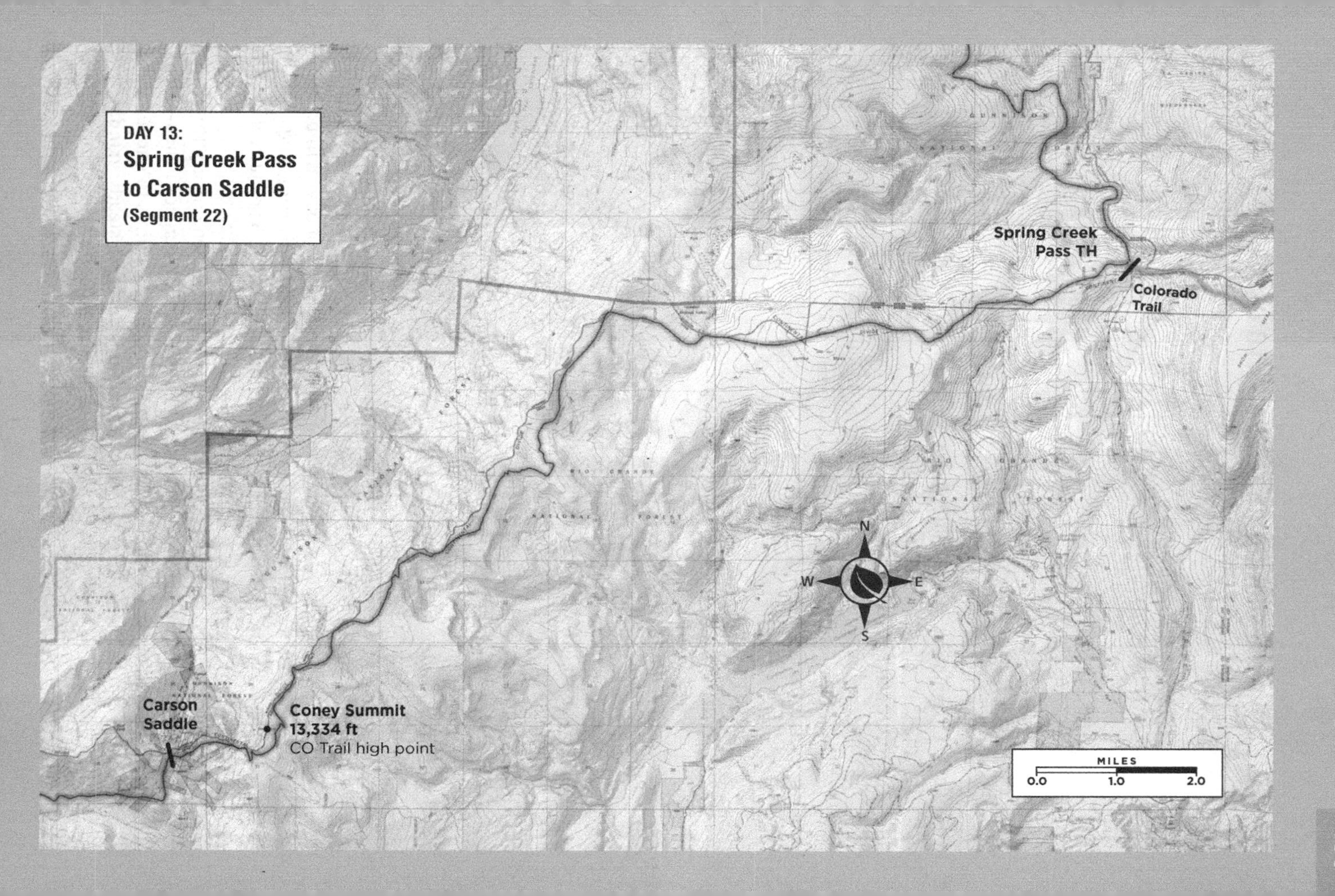
DAY 13:
Spring Creek Pass
to Carson Saddle
(Segment 22)
Spring Creek
Pass TH
Colorado
Trail
Coney Summit
13,334 ft
CO Trail high point
Carson
Saddle
N
W
E
S
MILES
0.0
1.0
2.0

DAY 13 SPRING CREEK PASS TO CARSON SADDLE SEGMENT 22

SEGMENT 22 = 17.2 miles
VERTICAL = 3,505

FUN FACTOR: 5
Today's ride has all the epic things: beauty, challenge, pucker—and the CT high point.

SUFFERFEST FACTOR: 5
Climbing at this altitude is hard.

PUCKER FACTOR: 4.5
According to my well-honed, panic-laced acrophobia, the steepest, rockiest, scariest, most exposed section of the entire Colorado Trail exists here.

BEAUTY FACTOR: 5
This is easily one of the most majestic segments of the entire CT.

SUFFER QUOTIENT: 2,691.

If I had to pick two segments that have the ability to change your life, to transform who you are and what your human purpose might be, two segments that will fill you with awe at the rugged, unkempt beauty of this planet, they would be Segments 22 and 23.

Looking at the information in the *Guidebook* and the vert maps, you might think yet again, *Easy, I can crank through both of those in one day*. And yes, you might. But the *Guidebook* doesn't quite prepare you for the exertion required to clear these next two segments.

Segment 22, while only 17 miles, features a series of climbs to the CT high point at 13,271 feet, just under Coney Summit. You'll spend most of the day above 12,500 feet, and the weather on the best of days will be cool and probably windy. It could also turn out to be deadly frigid and raining—or snowing—with angry, storm clouds all about. The entire day you'll feel as if you're on top of the world. And you kinda are.

The ride begins easy enough on a double-track, then quickly thins out to a singletrack crossing tundra filled with small, jagged, lichen-covered rocks. Since you won't have many reference points to gauge, you won't exactly notice that you're climbing, but it's a steady grind. Eventually, you'll reach the apex of the tundra, where a vast panorama opens up.

If there's one reason why you're out here, why you decided to ride this goddamn exhausting trail, this is perhaps it: an indescribably magnificent view, one that will make you feel very small in the world. This sight, reached only by consistent, brutal striving, will fill you with a hundred thoughts and feelings. You are here, on this planet, in this unique place, gazing upon a vista that few will ever see. You are doing something incredible, and no one will ever be able to take any of that away from you.

In other words, if all life is suffering, then the suffering is worth it, because you are in a place where nature is pure and solemn. And does not care one whit about you.

In other words: the view is freaking awesome. And a little scary.

The only time I got completely sketched out, when I panicked and thought *I can't go on,* occurred here on a very steep climb with several switchbacks. A frigid wind howled, and the trail ran straight up, with some epic exposure. Since I have a tiny bit of a fear of heights—okay, I get scared witless—I did not thrive in this moment. I got to one of the switchbacks along a sort of cliff and couldn't figure out how to get the bike turned around without tumbling over and falling what seemed like thousands and thousands of feet. I sat down awkwardly, clutching my stupid, heavy bike, afraid it, too, would tumble down the mountain. I considered turning back and crawling down the way I came, but that was just as sketchy.

I was stuck. Trapped at about 13,000 feet on a loose, rocky switchback, and hyperventilating.

Eventually, I calmed myself down and regained somewhat normal breathing. Reason seeped through the panic and I determined the best way to get past this awful mountainside switchback, even though I was feeling a bit of vertigo most likely due to the altitude and a fresh dose of adrenaline. With great effort—and with a crazy-person yell, like a shot putter tossing a 16 lb. shot—I flipped the bike's direction, balancing the behemoth on its rear wheel and spinning it around. Just making that happen boosted my confidence and told me that there was nothing I couldn't handle, a feeling I really needed right then.

I might have sworn at the trail, too—something like "Fuck you, you stupid ridiculous, impossible trail, I hate you, you will never conquer me ..."

Only the wind, the rocks, and the sky heard me, of course. There was not another soul around.

After that, I sort of assumed the CT high point would be right around the bend, but alas, I was fooled. There's a short downhill, and then another saddle. Eventually, your mind sort of numbs over—after perhaps letting out several more guttural litanies of swear words about how the trail is a big lie and how everything is a trick and where the hell is the stupid high-point marker, and then you might begin to worry that maybe you missed it, somehow, or maybe you're on the wrong trail, even though it would be next to impossible to have taken a wrong turn, as there are no other turns to take.

As tough as you might be, a mind can unravel in these moments. If you're riding solo, this dialogue is internal, and often weirdly robust, with lots of back-and-forth. If you're with a partner or in a group, the other(s) will either help keep you calm, or drive you to say mean, biting things that you'll probably later regret saying. The map-and-mileage person in your group—and there should always be such a person in a group setting like this, though whether they are good at this task is another question—should be able to keep you informed and on target, and should be able to give you confidently delivered updates on how far away the CT high point is. As perennial optimists, they might, however, produce a never-ending stream of little white lies, like "it's not too far" or "there's just a little up and then we'll be there" for several hours. It will be up to you to decide whether this sort of subterfuge is helpful, or if this person should be shoved off a cliff.

Mental breakdowns and group dynamics aside, today's landscape will be mesmerizing. Keep going. You will eventually reach the CT high point (I promise), and if you've watched any YouTube videos or seen photos, this moment will feel both familiar and surreal. Of course, it's just a wood post with a sign on it, and somehow that is an appropriate paradox. How can a single point on earth with so much meaning and beauty be celebrated with a tiny rectangular sign made of some kind of polymer?

If I may make a suggestion: take a moment. Consider how awesome you are and how hard you worked to get here. And how, just days ago, you were standing in a parking lot by Waterton Canyon, next to another, larger sign, and how you got to this place all on your own.

You made it. You are a Golden God! It's all downhill from here.

That's not true, of course. Prepare for more suffering, though the trail for the rest of the day is a nice ribbon of singletrack for the most part, and there are a few sweet downhills, all above treeline. There's another steep, hike-a-bike-with-switchbacks section close to a few trail junctions where you could, actually, take a wrong turn if you're not careful. Then, there's a long downhill down to some old mining ruins, and then the segment ends. You'll pick up Segment 23 off a dirt road and continue on, crossing a steep slope in a wide, absolutely majestic valley, toward several good campsites. There are multiple water sources close by, so these sites are a good place to kick back and reflect some more on the intensity you've just endured. Enjoy the amazing views from your campsite, and be on the lookout for wildlife, especially moose. Have a good dinner, settle in, and rest well, because tomorrow will also be a very big day.

One final thought: I can't predict how it'll be for you, but this part of the Colorado Trail, is something I'll remember for as long as I live. It's that special.

ABOVE Yes, it is true: Over the mountains there are more mountains.

ABOVE The prettiest campsite ever—just a few miles past Carson Saddle.

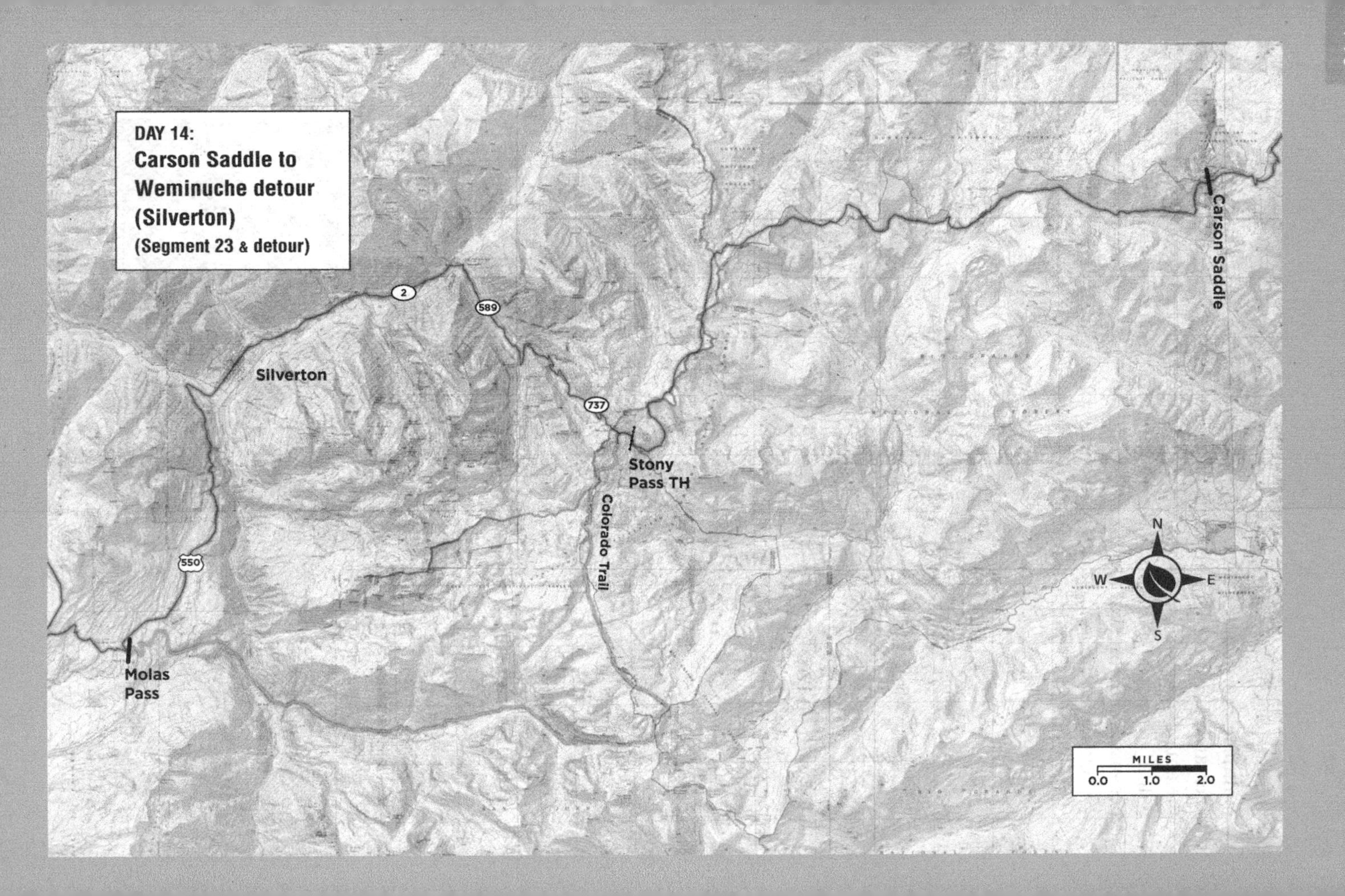

DAY 14:
Carson Saddle to
Weminuche detour
(Silverton)
(Segment 23 & detour)
Carson Saddle
Silverton
2
589
737
Stony
Pass TH
Colorado Trail
550
Molas
Pass
N
W
E
S
MILES
0.0
1.0
2.0

DAY 14 CARSON SADDLE TO WEMINUCHE DETOUR (SILVERTON) SEGMENT 23 & DETOUR

SEGMENT 23 = 13.9 miles
SILVERTON DETOUR = 10.8
TOTAL = 24.7
VERTICAL = 3,515

FUN FACTOR: 4.
Fun? More like amazement at the landscape and relief when you finally get to Stony Pass.

SUFFERFEST FACTOR: 5
It will be hard. Even the rugged downhill to Silverton will be painful, mostly on your hands—and brake pads.

PUCKER FACTOR: 4
A fair bit of exposure, good chance of scary storms, and that downhill into Silverton.

BEAUTY FACTOR: 5
Might be even prettier than Segment 22.

SUFFER QUOTIENT: 3,181—highest of the entire trip.

Today's sojourn is going to be similar to yesterday's, but harder, I'm not gonna lie. You'll climb over multiple—about eight or so—unnamed passes, each seemingly more challenging than the previous one.

Your three consolations will be thus:

1. **Each climb is followed by a short downhill.**

2. **The terrain and vistas are sublime. All above treeline, deeply green, rugged, rocky, sky everywhere, alpine lakes, tall peaks. And perhaps a flock or two of sheep.**

3. **You'll end the day in Silverton, having survived the most remote part of the colorado trail.**

I don't think it matters how tough, how in-shape, or how massive your quads are, Segment 23 will take some time. You're not going to set any speed records, which is as it should be. There's really no reason to rush through; I urge you to *just be* in this incredible landscape, to stop and look around—often. You'll be sucking some serious wind anyway, so take time to catch your breath and take lots of pictures and video. You'll want a record of where you are and what you're accomplishing. Soon enough you'll hit Stony Pass and then descend on a rough and crazy road into Silverton.

The first climb is long, slow, and not too bad. The valley itself so dang beautiful it should make the slog a little easier. And by slog, as I said before, I mean you will encounter on this day a multitude of false summits; so stay focused and don't get discouraged, just keep on keeping on, as Bob Dylan is fond of singing. There will be a fairly regular cycle of climbing on the bike; hiking with the bike; inch-worming with the bike; standing and sucking wind at the top of yet another saddle; a downhill jaunt that never seems to last very long. Stay hydrated, eat your nourishment, and be careful. When you're beat tired at this altitude brain fog is a real thing, and you can easily do something stupid, like dump some fresh spring water into your camelback before treating it—something I did so nonchalantly I had to sit and think a bit about what had just happened and how I would fix it. Luckily, I had some iodine tablets packed away.

Which are disgusting, by the way.

There are many hard things about riding the CT—the heat of the early sections, the steepness of Gold Hill, Sargents Mesa's ludicrous rockiness, and so on. But for absolute difficulty, Segment 23 might take the award. And yet, eventually it'll be over and you'll find yourself missing the challenge and beauty of it all.

Toward the end of the day, I was pretty spent. As I got close to Stony Pass, crossing over a saddle and rolling a short bit of trail that serpentines back and forth before dropping into a huge valley, rain began falling, the wind howled, but there was bright sun in the distance. I dropped into a valley, and suddenly the wind disappeared. Ahead, there must have been a thousand grazing sheep; their bleats were both comforting and hilarious. Three shepherding dogs ran up the steep face of a ridge across from me, nudging large groups of unruly sheep back down into the main herd. A shepherd, high up in the meadow, walked slowly down the valley, whistling and hollering commands at the dogs. Their symbiosis was charming, a kind of coordinated dance. Several enormous Great Pyrenees lazed in various haphazard locations; sheep stood around them, like groupies. Eventually, they, too, got moving, though very slowly.

I rode alongside the flock, above them on the valley's slope, toward Stony Pass Road. I was so happy when I got to the road, I cried a little.

And then I did something really, really stupid.

ABOVE Photos do not accurately represent the beauty of this landscape.

I'd been studying the *Guidebook* for days, so I didn't think I needed to check one more time. Of course I knew where I was going. *Of course.*

I got to the road and turned left, downhill. *I'm on my way to Silverton! I'm almost done!* I thought, and I began singing "Rocky Mountain High" as I flew down that dirt road at an outrageous speed.

I should point out here: when you get to Stony Pass Road, you're supposed to *turn right and climb* to the top of Stony Pass before descending into Silverton.

I'd made a terrible mistake. Something I didn't realize until the road leveled out and I met a few off-roaders taking a break. About four miles down from the pass.

I won't say any more about that here; the complete story is just ahead.

If you're not stupid like me and turn right to ride to the top of Stony Pass, the roll down into Silverton is hair-raising. It's long, steep, and loose. It may be crowded with 4-wheelers as well.

Silverton, much like Leadville, is a cool little place that hasn't been commodified into the typical Colorado tourist/ski-town. It has a haphazard feel to it, which is to say that it still embraces its roots as a rough-and-tumble mining town. I'd suggest getting a room with a real bed, eating to your heart's content, and drinking a few cold brews before embarking on the final push to Durango. There's still a fair amount of hard work ahead, but you're going to have a great time. I promise.

ABOVE Old mining towns like Silverton typically have their own unique culture—and sense of humor.

GRUB IN SILVERTON

Bent Elbow Saloon: awesome breakfast.
Brown Bag Silverton: great sandwiches.
Golden Block Brewery: cold beer, hot pizza, both very tasty.

BIKE SHOPS

Pedal the Peaks
906 Greene Street

Fall Line Sports
302 Lewis Street

PLACES TO STAY: There are a several good choices, from super-cheap to high end.

Avon Hotel
Cool historic, rustic, lots of typewriters, awesome bar and lobby, owners are super nice. My personal fave.
144 East 10th St, Silverton, CO 81433
303-910-2960
www.avonsilverton.com

Kendall Mountain Lodge
Formerly a hostel, rustic, simple, everyone there is super nice. Cheap.
1025 Blair Street Silverton, CO 81433
970) 844-6465
www.kendallmountainlodge.com

Red Mountain Motel and RV Park
Basic, no frills. Cheap.
664 Green St, Silverton, CO 81433
888-970-5512
redmtmotelrvpk.com

Prospector Motel
No frills, easy to store bike in your room. Cheap.
1015 Greene St, Silverton, CO 81433
970-387-5466
www.prospectormotel.com

Grand Imperial Hotel
Very fancy, cool history, dizzying wallpaper, and doilies. Not cheap.
1219 Greene Street, Silverton, CO 81433
970-367-4120
www.grandimperialhotel.com

Teller House Hotel
Also historic, though less doily-filled. Not cheap.
1250 Greene Street, Silverton, CO 81433
970-387-5423
tellerhouse.com

7 OVER THE MOUNTAIN THERE ARE MORE MOUNTAINS

First published in Elevation Outdoors, *November 2018*

After a week of bikepacking the Colorado Trail, pedaling, walking, crawling from the base of Mount Princeton on my way to Silverton, when I finally glimpsed the golden ribbon of Stony Pass Road I was so overcome with joy I admit I cried. My spent muscles trembled with adrenaline and I pedaled my Stumpjumper, loaded with camping gear, along a very thin single-track. I tried to focus on the hazardous terrain under my tires but was distracted by hundreds of sheep in the high-alpine valley below, all bleating a one-note chorus. It was a miraculous thing to behold.

Two border collies sprinted up steep treeless hillsides, harassing fluffy white dots of recalcitrant sheep, organizing them into a coherent flock and nudging them down the valley. A shepherd followed the congregation, calling and whistling commands. And like any typical afternoon in the high mountains, there was brilliant blue sky and rain, dark ominous clouds and a rainbow. I reveled in the beauty of the moment, completely exhausted, completely ecstatic. In my next life, I thought, I want to come back as a shepherd. Tears came to my eyes. Good ones. There are, after all, many ways a man can cry, and biking the Colorado Trail will bring out them all.

Let me be the first to tell you: Pushing 60 pounds of bike and gear in stiff bike shoes really sucks. I'd read somewhere that the truth of

LEFT One more bridge.
ABOVE When you get to Taylor Lake, you're almost done. Almost.

bikepacking the Colorado Trail is this: You can ride about 80 percent, but you won't spend 80 percent of your time riding. The last two days I'd spent just a couple of hours in the saddle, covering about 40 miles and climbing over 8,000 feet. Contrary to recent noise about how the CT is the most awesome 535-mile bikepacking trail, it's really made for hiking. Who knew? Well, I do now.

I'm 51 years old. I knew riding the Colorado Trail would be hard. Last summer I'd bikepacked from Waterton Canyon to Leadville; I'd planned to finish the Trail on this second sojourn, rolling into Durango, the western terminus, a dirty, rank, self-made hero. I'd decided on this endeavor after a cancer scare two winters ago. I'd had this old injury—a calf muscle tear that had developed into a knot which I'd always believed was just scar tissue. I went to a sports doc, who then referred me to a limb surgeon, who then referred me to an oncologist. The surgeon removed the malignant mass, leaving me with a five-inch scar. And all that time I never really worried. Even after the diagnosis, while awaiting the full-body MRI and chest CT results I was like, Eh, no big deal. My wife, however, worried enough for the both of us. And luckily, all the tests came back negative.

I thought I'd ride the trail to further confirm that, yes, I was okay. I was still the guy who thrived on difficult physical challenges, something I've been doing since junior high cross-country. I enjoy the pain, the pushing of one's body and mind to a breaking point, and past. Mountain biking hurts, it scares me, it makes me feel alive. And Colorado is a most fabulous landscape in which to perform these experiments.

The road loomed in the distance, tantalizing, entrancing, promising an easy downhill into Silverton and a night of sleep in a real bed. And cold beer! And pizza! And a chance to take a shower—my first in a week. And an opportunity to restock my food cache.

I rolled over a few more ridges and then the road quickly rose to meet the descending trail, and I was out. Done. Finished with the single-track. No more hike-a-bike. No more stressing about food or water. I'd been walking my bike for most of the last two days, unrideable climb after unrideable climb, most of it above treeline, around 12,000 feet in altitude. A sun shower began to fall, lighting the peaks around me in a silvery glow. I turned my bike left, pointed the front wheel downhill, and away I went. The trail wasn't as rocky as the guidebooks had promised, but I was glad and thought nothing of it. I flew downhill, singing John Denver's "Rocky Mountain High" at top volume, perhaps slightly off key. The feeling was pure bliss, endorphin high, relief. Again, I might have teared up just a bit.

Then, a river crossing appeared. I didn't remember the guidebook saying anything about a river. My phone was dead, so I couldn't check my GPS app. Had I missed a turn somewhere? I dismounted and stomped through the stream, soaking my feet. I was so loopy and stupefied from the last two days of effort, I couldn't understand why I hadn't made it to Silverton already. Oh, Silverton, why hast thou forsaken me?

I reached a road junction, and a guy in a Jeep pulled up. I waved to him and he stopped. "Hey, do you know which way leads to Silverton?"

"It's that way. Up and over the pass," he said, pointing up the road I'd just bombed down.

Right then I remembered: When the trail reaches the road you're supposed to turn *right, uphill*, for about two-tenths of a mile, and *then* you cruise downhill into Silverton. I recalled the passage in the guidebook, which I'd read about a hundred times over the past few days, huddled in my tent in the dusk light before falling asleep, grubby and bone tired.

Oh no. No, no, no.

"I went the wrong way," I said. "Oh crud. I can't ride back up that." I bent over and put my hands on my knees as if I might puke.

And then the thing that often happens out on the trail, when you're out in the middle of nowhere and in dire straits, when you're about to give up: a fellow human saves your dumb ass.

"I'm going that way, I can take you," Jeep dude said.

When he said that, I cried again. But just a little bit. On the inside.

His name was Jake and he drove a super-cool tricked-out new Jeep with massive, pillowy tires and a rack on top, where he stowed my bike. He carted me over the pass and into Silverton. I promptly procured a room at the funky and friendly Avon Hotel. I took a long shower, went out for dinner, ate an entire pizza, drank two beers, and collapsed into a soft, clean bed.

The next morning, I woke up in Silverton and didn't want to get out of bed. When I finally did, the mere act of walking proved a challenge, and when I thought of the remaining 80 miles and 13,000 feet of climbing, I crawled back into bed. And when I thought of my lovely wife and two amazing teenage daughters and our cute little house, and yes, even our weird dog who digs random holes all over the back yard, I was overwhelmed by homesickness. It was then I really cried. I mean I wept. It was a mixture of happiness and loneliness and relief and amazement and a bunch of other emotions. Right then I decided that my adventure was over. Durango could wait until next summer.

My week on the Trail confirmed many truths—truths one can only learn while in high mountains. There's beauty that is unspeakably profound, beauty not many will ever see in person, beauty I'll not soon forget. Often, the most difficult efforts are the most worthy, but while you're in it, it's misery. Pushing my bike up a steep, loose slope, storms raging all around, my breath ragged, my energy reserves on empty, I was definitely miserable. But when I'd gotten somewhere—I couldn't have been happier. In eight days, I'd traveled over 200 miles. I'd forged enduring memories. I'd confirmed that I was, in fact, okay—even though I'd gone the wrong way, even though I'd sometimes walked when I could have ridden, even though I'd decided I was done.

I made some calls and procured a rental car back to Denver. The drive home, with the windows down and stereo cranked up loud, definitely felt like a step in the right direction. And yes, I cried.

ABOVE Sometimes the journey looks like a metaphor for one's life. Sometimes you're not sure where you're going, but you keep moving forward, always forward.

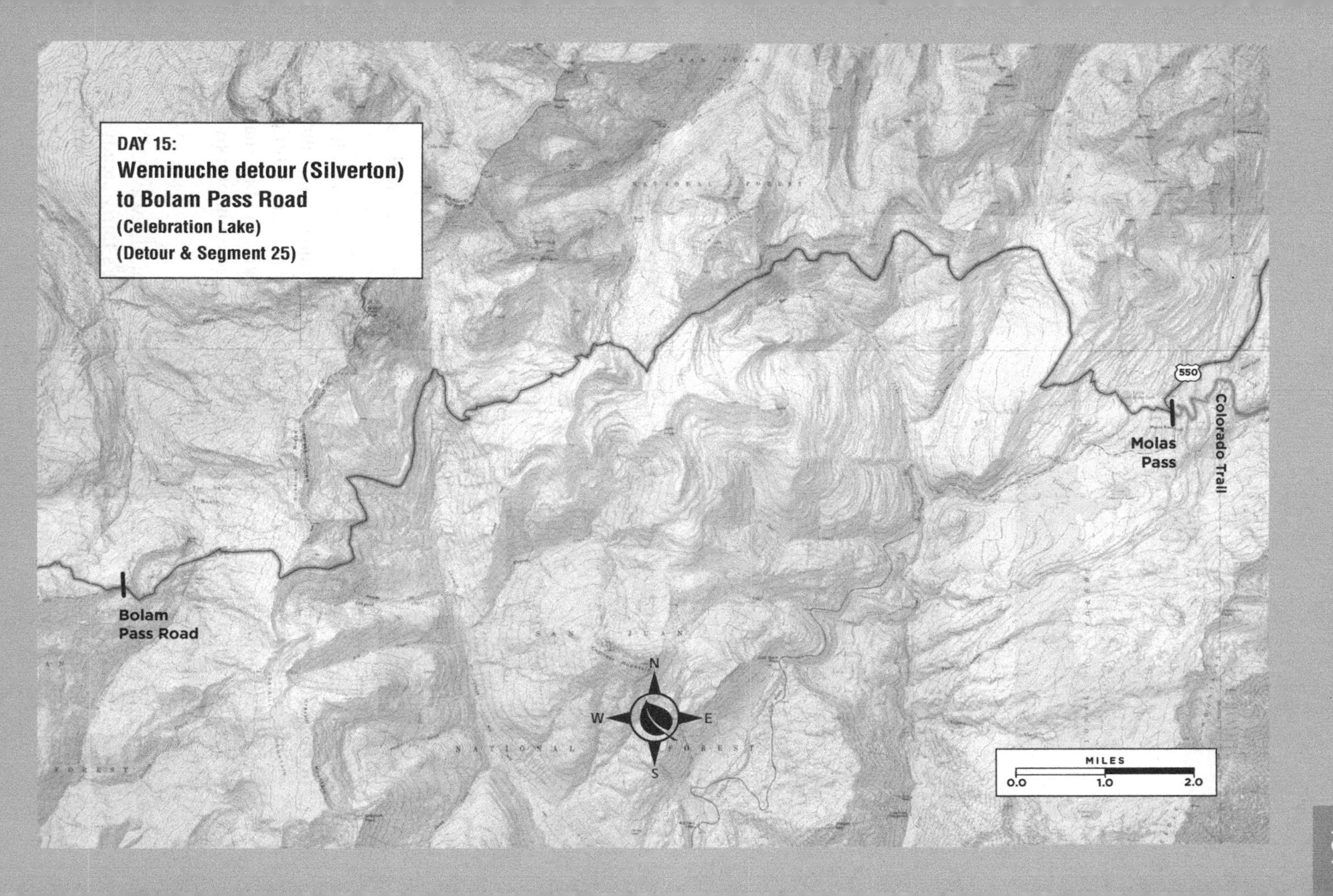
DAY 15:
Weminuche detour (Silverton)
to Bolam Pass Road
(Celebration Lake)
(Detour & Segment 25)
550
Colorado Trail
Molas Pass
Bolam Pass Road
N
W
E
S
MILES
0.0
1.0
2.0

DAY 15 WEMINUCHE DETOUR (SILVERTON) TO BOLAM PASS ROAD (CELEBRATION LAKE) DETOUR & SEGMENT 25

WEMINUCHE DETOUR = 5.7 miles
SEGMENT 25 = 20.9
TOTAL = 26.6
VERTICAL = 1,582 + 3,799 = 5,381

FUN FACTOR: 4
Great riding, not a ton of hike-a-bike.

SUFFERFEST FACTOR: 4
Lots of climbing, but it's more the quantity, and not the steepness, that make it a challenge.

PUCKER FACTOR: 2.5
Not much to worry about.

BEAUTY FACTOR: 5
You're back in the high mountains.

SUFFER QUOTIENT: 2,200

Now, what you've already ridden on this sojourn—and hiked, crawled, et cetera—has been pretty amazing, am I right? You've experienced a brilliant mix of buttery singletrack, killer climbs, savage downhills, rock gardens, windy tundra, long cruiser sections, dirt road, mountain-town main streets, dense forest, open vistas.

The trail that lies between here and Durango is going to make all that pale in comparison.

Okay, maybe that's a bit of hyperbole—the entire CT is a tableau of inspiring beauty and ruggedness. Silverton to Durango is just more of that, with perhaps a little more color, a little more majesty, a little more everything. To be sure some of this has to do with the fact that you're on the last stretch, and can feel the closeness of an impressive accomplishment: Colorado Trail Completer.

Or should I say: Survivor?

Leaving Silverton, there's a good uphill grind on highway 550—about 1,500 feet in all, but as most road climbs go, it's fairly steady and there's a good shoulder to ride on. Your reward is an unbelievably breathtaking view at the CT Molas Pass trailhead. Definitely take a

ABOVE Enter here for some sweet riding.

moment, enjoy your early accomplishment—getting back to the trail—before rolling back onto the dirt, the dirt that will take you to Durango. You could also save some singletrack-riding energy and get a lift up to the trailhead. There's nothing wrong with that.

The route here is a nice mix of up and down, and the riding is sweet. Tall mountains all around, fields of wildflowers, big sky, and rideable dirt. What more could you ask for? You'll encounter several lakes and waterfalls, along with some incredible mountains, including Engineer Mountain and Lizard Head Peak. There will be some steeps that are hike-a-bike, but not as many as you experienced the day before, or the day before that. About 10 miles in you will most likely encounter some snow fields that are easily traversed, but pretty wild nonetheless, considering that you'll be walking through the white stuff in the middle of summer. Even though I'm from Buffalo, New York, and therefore intimately familiar with snow, seeing it, walking on it, making snowballs in July/August is just surreal.

You'll also encounter lots of climbing, and this is why, though today's mileage seems paltry, it will take you a while, and if you stayed in Silverton, you might want to get a leisurely start, after a hearty breakfast in town. Also, today's itinerary builds in some extra time for relaxing and enjoying the scenery. Think less slog, less grind, less death march, and more ride. Who wants to be in a hurry to finish, anyway?

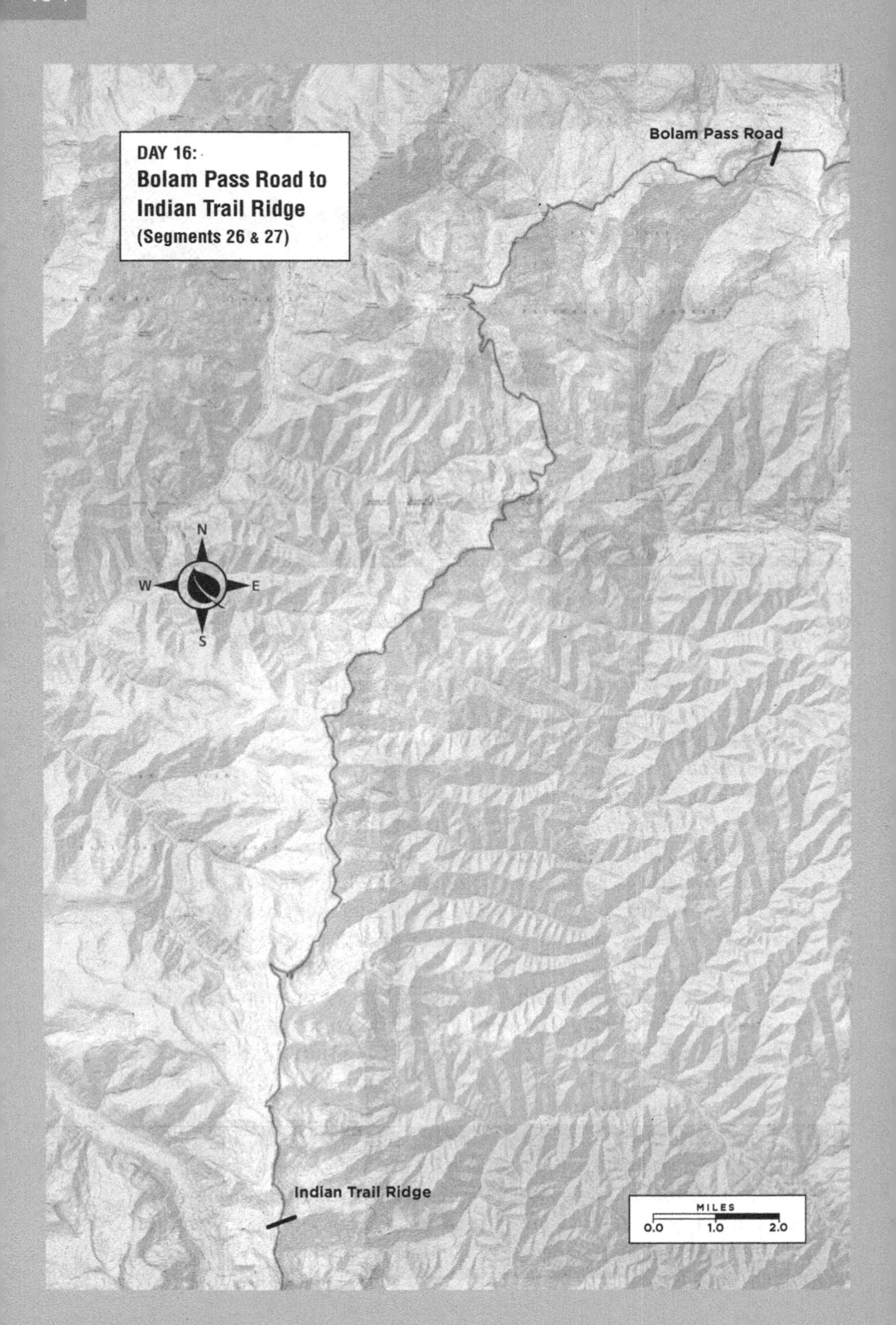
DAY 16:
Bolam Pass Road to
Indian Trail Ridge
(Segments 26 & 27)
Bolam Pass Road
N
W
E
S
Indian Trail Ridge
MILES
0.0
1.0
2.0

DAY 16 BOLAM PASS ROAD TO BASE OF INDIAN TRAIL RIDGE SEGMENTS 26 & 27

SEGMENT 26 = 10.9 miles
SEGMENT 27 = 12.3
TOTAL = 23.2
VERTICAL = 1,827 + 1,344 = 3,171

FUN FACTOR: 4
Kind of a repeat of yesterday.

SUFFERFEST FACTOR: 3.0
Totally manageable day. You'll feel like a normal biker for the most part.

PUCKER FACTOR: 2.5
Not much to worry about.

BEAUTY FACTOR: 5

SUFFER QUOTIENT: 1,528

"Beauty is truth, truth beauty,"—that is all
Ye know on earth, and all ye need to know.

—John Keats

Today's ride will feel like a picnic, and you might be tempted to see if you can make it all the way through Segment 27 to Taylor Lake. That's certainly possible, but be forewarned: Indian Trail Ridge, which is about five miles long, is infamous for lightning and vicious weather. If there's any chance of storms moving in, stay off this section. It's above treeline, it's exposed, rocky, and almost always windy. If you're going to combine days on the way from Silverton to Durango, it would be best to continue past Bolam Pass/Celebration Lake, yesterday's destination, and see how close you can get to Indian Trail Ridge. If you do that, you could make this last bit from Silverton to Durango in two days instead of three.

Back to the topic of Indian Trail Ridge. Here's a true story: While on my ride, I had the honor of meeting Jerry Brown, the first person

ABOVE The top of Engineer Pass.

to ever bikepack the CT and the main surveyor of the Trail, at Spring Creek Pass. When I asked him for advice about the trail ahead, the one piece of advice he gave was this: Be careful on Indian Trail Ridge. There are almost always thunderstorms in the afternoon, and they're almost always packing serious lightning.

Todays' ride will take you close to where the Indian Trail Ridge climb begins in earnest. Tomorrow, if you get up at a normal hour and get a-ridin', you should reach the Ridge's high point early in the day and will hopefully avoid being zapped by an angry bolt from Zeus. Stopping before Indian Trail Ridge makes today, Day 16, a piece of cake, a walk in the park, a relaxing jaunt. Soon enough, you'll be in Durango and stuck back in the world of commerce and cars and demands and annoying people.

As the day progresses, you'll begin climbing up toward Blackhawk Pass, which is one of the prettiest places on earth, and pretty dang rideable. You'll roll through riches of wildflowers, and then on the last pitch the views open to mountains striated with brilliant golds and reds.

After crossing over Blackhawk Pass, the ride continues to be high fun-factor. The trail levels out and follows a long ridgeline, filled with color, especially green. The weight of your bike will somehow lessen here, and you'll roll along like you'd normally would when out for an afternoon ride. Feel free to take a few extra breaks, maybe take an afternoon nap if the weather is good.

ABOVE The wildflowers around Blackhawk Pass are insanely pretty.

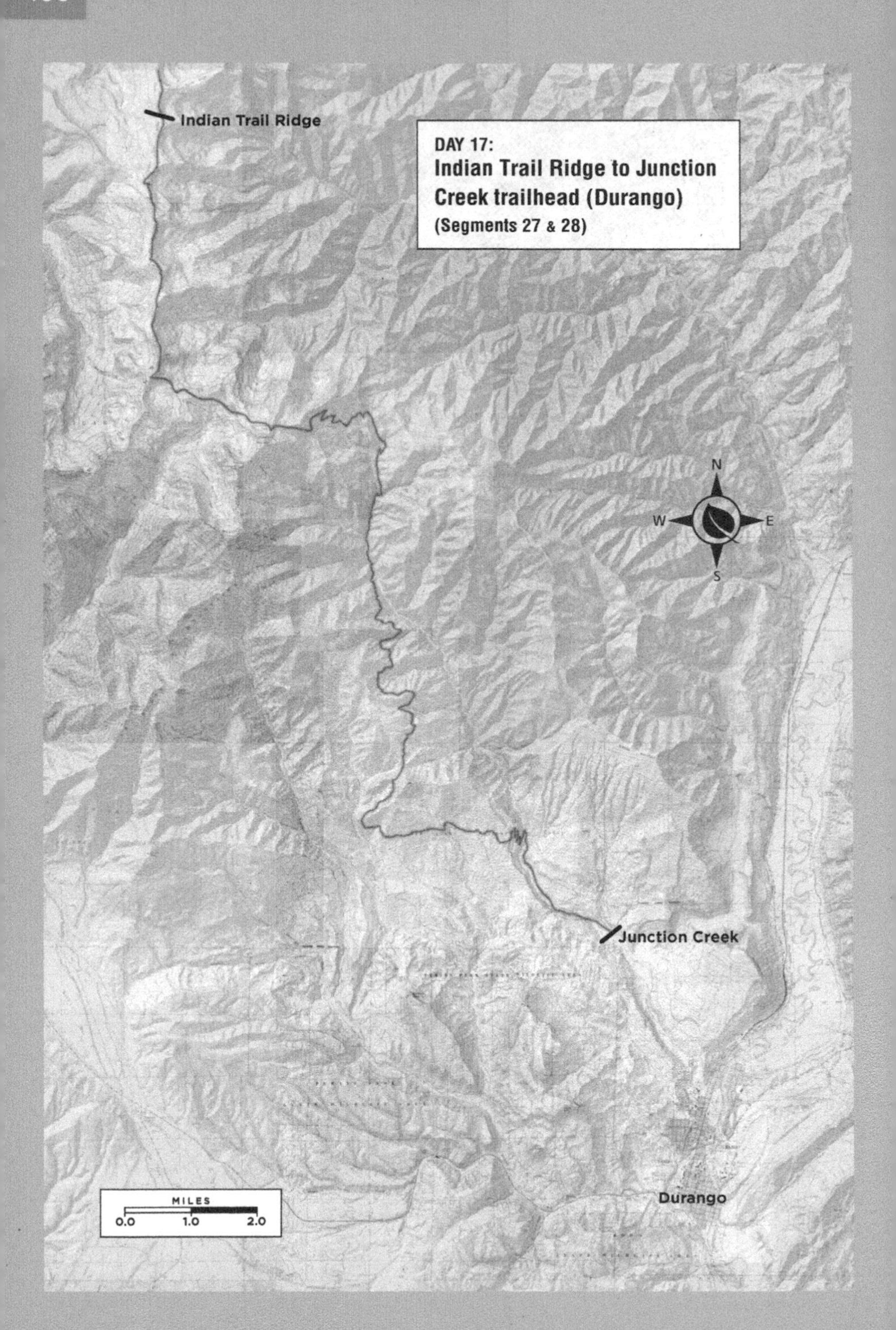
Indian Trail Ridge
DAY 17:
Indian Trail Ridge to Junction Creek trailhead (Durango)
(Segments 27 & 28)
N
W
E
S
Junction Creek
Durango
MILES
0.0
1.0
2.0

DAY 17 INDIAN TRAIL RIDGE TO JUNCTION CREEK TRAILHEAD (DURANGO) SEGMENTS 27 & 28

SEGMENT 27 = 8.3 miles
SEGMENT 28 = 21.5
TO DURANGO = 3.5
TOTAL = 33.3
VERTICAL = 2,842 + 1,897 = 4,739

FUN FACTOR: 5
Your last day! Two pretty decent climbs, one massive downhill. Are your brakes in good shape?

SUFFERFEST FACTOR: 4
It's a long day, with pretty much everything: ascents, scrambles, weather, sketchy downhills, mileage.

PUCKER FACTOR: 4
Some exposure, chunky rock fields, and loose downhills.

BEAUTY FACTOR: 5
The view from Indian Trail Ridge is sublime.

SUFFER QUOTIENT: 1,343

Today, your final day, is bittersweet. It will be hard. It will be very picturesque. It will be long. It will probably be a little stressful, and certainly emotional. And then you'll be done. You'll re-enter your regular life and the vaguely familiar, complicated world, leaving the Trail and your simple, one-directional, two-wheeled existence.

Re-entry is never easy, but I do think that, on the final day, you can begin preparing. Keep in mind that while your ride is ending, you will forever carry the Colorado Trail within you—in your memories and dreams, in the way you see the world, and in how you see yourself. You'll stand tall, with a little more pride, a little more patience, a little more confidence. You might have a calmer perspective, understanding that the usual annoying challenges in one's day aren't really all that terrible. You'll know in your heart that the essential, true things of this world are simple and elemental: earth, sky, air, sun, moon, water. Your loved ones—those people you've missed desperately because yes, absence does make the heart grow fonder—will be even more dear to you. While out on the Trail you'll come to understand that they are the most important things, and you will make a promise to yourself to make sure they stay close to you, because you love them deeply and always will.

I don't want to make this final day into some sort overwhelming epiphany-fest, and I'm not suggesting you ride while being endlessly moved by how much love and appreciation you have in your heart. Yet I do think it's okay to feel a host of emotions—as I surely did.

I suggest getting up early, since it will not only be a long day, but also weather on Indian Trail Ridge can undoubtedly be dangerous. Try to navigate the Ridge before the typical afternoon storms roll in. The trail that leads there is pretty and not too challenging. You'll ride some and walk some, but it's not a terrible slog.

So yes, you'll climb for a while and eventually get to Indian Trail Ridge, which itself is super cool, seeing as it's a five-mile long, narrow, rock-strewn ridge with grand vistas in all directions, meandering up and over several saddles and peaks before eventually—and rather suddenly, I must say—opening up to a rocky, cliffside descent (which I completely walked down, by the way) above Taylor Lake. Basically, once you see Taylor Lake, you're getting close. Just be aware and don't get too excited early on—there are several false summits along the way.

I was lucky on my ride. When I reached Indian Trail Ridge there

ABOVE Indian Trail Ridge will remind you of the CT high point, miles back.

was nary a cloud in the sky. It was mildly windy and the temperature was perfect—about 70 degrees. It was probably the best day I'd had out on the CT, maybe because I knew I was almost done, but also because I could see for miles and miles in every direction.

The view of Taylor Lake is unbelievably pretty and majestic, and a kind of visual paradox: the massive, sharp mountains above Taylor Lake are far away, and yet the perspective makes everything look like a miniature diorama. If the weather is clear, you'll see it all: rugged peaks, blue water, jeep trails meandering up into the wilds and disappearing into folds of rock, and the Colorado Trail—a thin line through fields of wildflowers, drawing your eye past Taylor Lake and up to Kennebec Pass. Once you survive the steep, exposed pitch down toward Taylor Lake, you'll ride through a valley with wildflowers up to your ears. It's likely a place where you'll encounter some humanity—more than you've seen in quite a while. I'd posit that this is a welcome sight. We tend to be happy to see other humans after not being around them for a while, and especially when meeting up by a mesmerizing lake and meadow.

Once you reach Kennebec Pass, think about this: you're going to drop about 6,000 feet in elevation over the course of the next 20 miles. Somewhere ahead lies the iconic Colorado Trail sign outside of Durango. Just a few more hours and you'll be there.

ABOVE More wildflowers.

But first: there's an easy, though tiring, climb up to Kennebec Pass, and then a long, freaky, steep decent on loose shale. I chickened out and did not ride this part. Some of you will be able to ride it, but give yourself a break if you end up like me. Nobody wants to slide hundreds of feet down a scree field of sharp rocks on the final day of the ride of a lifetime. Either way, be safe, stay in control, and keep eating up trail. After all, that's your goal: to finish. No one's going to care what you rode, how fast you went (unless you're racing), what you walked or what you cleaned.

After the scree field, hop back on your bike and hold on, for you are going down, man. You'll enter some woods, and it's awesome. You'll pass the Gaines Gulch waterfall, which is also awesome. You'll cross over Junction Creek a bunch of times. If you're from Colorado, the trail here will feel a little, well, Front Range-y. In some ways it's a lot like the singletrack by Waterton Canyon—narrow, rocky, and lush with green.

Until you reach the last climb of your sojourn. Which, I must say, I did not enjoy very much.

ABOVE Looking back up the scree field past Kennebec Pass.

I was totally spent by then, and as I've said before, I'm not a fan of exposure. The trail here, while not totally on a cliff, is fairly steep, exposed, narrow, and—this is mostly what did me in—off camber. (By the way, the scree field right after Kennebec Pass is also off camber.) I lost my nerve and could not get into climbing mode. Again, some riders won't even think twice about it. If you're one of those ledge-walking-totally-chill persons, I admire you.

The climb seems to go on forever, even though it's just a couple of miles. Toward the end of the uphill, the trail slides away from the steeps, and the riding is brilliant. You'll eventually reach a broad turn in the trail with good views, and it'll be apparent that the climbing is over, finally. *Finally!*

I seem to remember a pickaxe stuck in the ground right about there, but cannot confirm this. I wish I'd taken a photo of the damn thing. Maybe I imagined it?

Here's where you'll crush any hikers that you've been chasing. The trail is mostly flowy through Aspen and Pine forests, and the riding is generally fast and fun.

When your reach Gudy's Rest, stop and take a moment to contemplate not only the view, but what you've accomplished. Remind yourself that you've done an incredible thing. Remember all the suffering and joys you've experienced, all the stresses and breakdowns and epiphanies and deep insights. Holler into the canyon, pat yourself on the back, have a good cry. Do whatever feels right.

But before you continue on, also give a prayerful thank you to Gudy Gaskill, who helped make the Colorado Trail become a reality. She worked tirelessly to build this outdoor sanctuary (torture chamber?), a place to find yourself and the inexpressible miracle of being, except this sanctuary is not a building with an altar and stained glass, it's a holy pathway that runs about 500 miles, with a roof of sky and a majesty that captivates. Feel all the love for everything you care about, feel the love of this opportunity, for this experience you've had and for all those who've helped you get here. Give thanks to it all.

And then get ready for more wild elevation loss.

At places this last stretch feels like an enduro course—big, bermed turns, tight switchbacks, drops galore. You may think the finish is closer than it is at a couple of points, but no bother, you know how to cover distance. (This was also a place where I was glad to have a full-squish bike.)

Suddenly the trail levels out and you'll emerge from a copse of trees and you'll see a parking lot and the CT triptych sign will appear, inauspiciously standing to the left of the trail. Make sure to take an absolute ton of pictures. And celebrate!

However, if no one is there with balloons, cold beer, champagne, and maybe a big fat smooch, it might feel a little anticlimactic. When I got there, it was late in the day—around 6 PM. A guy was sitting on a big rock at the edge of the parking lot, and that was pretty much it. None of my loved ones were there to witness my finishing—they were all in Denver, New York, California, and Buffalo, going about their days. And I rode alone, so there was no commiseration or deep feelings of brotherhood, sisterhood, or personhood to be had. I asked the guy sitting on the rock if he would take my picture in front of the Colorado Trail sign. He happily obliged.

And that was it. I rode into town and bought a pair of bargain sandals at the supermarket, found a cheap motel room, ordered Pizza Hut, watched some baseball on TV, and fell asleep around 10 PM. In a way it was both a transcendent and kind of lame day, accomplishing something I'd dreamed about for five years, something I suffered mightily through, something that taught me I was tougher than I often think I am, something that I knew I'd be pondering for the rest of my life. And yet, the pizza guy was just a pizza guy, and the sun set and rose the next morning, and no one seemed to look at me differently. When I got home, my wife and kids were more excited about the box of Palisade peaches I'd brought home than the heroic endeavor I'd just completed.

ABOVE It's all over. Kind of bittersweet.

But you know what? That's just fine. After all, riding the Colorado Trail is something you're going to do for you and no one else, and probably no one would understand anyway. Except maybe another bikepacker who's completed the whole damn thing.

If you're riding into Durango from the western terminus, you've got about four miles of quiet paved roads. It'll probably feel a little dreamlike. In fact, the next several days will feel that way. Re-entry is often a little strange. Everything tends to seem a little unreal, and you might find yourself questioning the necessity of things around you—coffeemakers, tables, TVs, news shows, cars.

Try to keep that feeling. I think it helps you remember what's absolutely integral, and what is merely distraction.

ABOVE Waiting at the train station in Durango. Seems like that would make a good song, or poem, title.

ABOVE Taylor Lake.

INTERVIEWS

BEN HANDRICH AND ANDY BRUBAKER

"You find yourself sometimes asking, why is this where the trail is? These highs and lows come so quickly, and the highs can be so high that you're convinced you're unstoppable, and the lows can be so low that you think you're about to die. There were times it made zero sense for me to be feeling really good, but I was feeling amazing."

—Payson McElveen,
as recorded in a YouTube video,
"Discovery and Despair on the Colorado Trail,"
in reference to his fastest known time
(FKT) attempt in 2020

In my ride prep, one of the things I did was watch a lot of YouTube videos. There are enough to entertain for many hours and get you super stoked. Every summer more appear, and while some are mere entertainment, they often contain important bits information about trail conditions—and provide a glimpse of what it's really like out there.

Of all the various videos, my favorites were Ryan VanDuzer's 2021 ride, along with another collection produced by Ben Handrich and Andy Brubaker, two young bucks with a plan—and a drone. I watched their videos dozens of times. Even now I sometimes watch them while training on a stationary bike in the basement. They are honest, they are funny, they are inspiring, and the videography is stunning. (Ryan's videos are pretty great, too. I especially like how he doesn't shy away from the struggle of hike-a-biking.) I used Ben and Andy's little end-of-the-day analyses to mentally prepare for my own ride. In many ways, their storytelling gave me vicarious wisdom ahead of time—wisdom that came in very handy once I hit the dirt.

Ben and Andy were kind enough to allow me to interview them. Here's what they had to say—first Ben, then Andy.

BEN HANDRICH INTERVIEW

What made you want to try this endeavor?
My friend Andy and I were just getting serious about bikepacking and had done part of the CT two years prior. We knew we needed to head back and do the whole thing in one go.

Overall, did you enjoy riding the CT?
That's a complicated question, but the short answer is ABSOLUTELY. It is an unforgettable experience for sure. Of course, there were moments. I had one pretty bad crash that had me sore the next day, which was just after leaving Buena Vista—that one had me thinking about remoteness and my lack of first-aid skills.

And when we were out in the middle of the San Juans, Andy had a major bonk one afternoon, which led to him struggling to eat enough the next day AND forgetting to bring his clothes into the tent that night. It rained all night, of course. Actually, we got rained on all three days in the San Juans to Silverton, and that bonk was the day before Silverton, so we were already pretty defeated by the perma-rain of the previous two days. Once we got to Silverton, though, a huge ultra-endurance running event was taking place the next day and we were completely re-inspired by all of the svelte athletes filling the restaurants and stores around Silverton. As we ate pizza and drank beer, Andy confessed that he was planning to call it once we got to Silverton but had a change of heart after food, a shower, and a really lucky situation where we were able to stay at a hostel despite it being full and all the hotels being full as well with the huge event happening the next day.

But the overall experience: priceless. The views, the storms, the trails conditions (the good and the horrible alike), it feels like a true adventure despite it being a somewhat accessible trail overall.

When you look back at your experience, what comes to mind?
Andy and I had a lot of fun videoing the experience together, and whenever we would sit down to hash out the day's ride with the GoPro, it was actually a great way to relive the best moments of the day and relive the moments where we were most present while riding, eating, adventuring, falling, persevering, and discussing.

Would you do it again?
I would. In fact, a friend from Oregon was planning to do it this year

and I almost jumped in with him, but it didn't work with my schedule. That being said, if the opportunity arises, I'll definitely get out there and give it a go.

Overall, how many days did you take to finish?
Andy and I did it in 13 days, but I think we could have done it in 11 or 12 pretty easily, if we hadn't been carrying so much drone and GoPro stuff. But it's definitely a hard trail, and I think most people should plan for at least two weeks to complete it.

Did you train a lot? What was your training regimen?
At the time I was just getting into ultra-endurance riding. My plan had been to yo-yo the route and head back out on the trail for the race after taking a week to recover from our touring pace. However, after finishing, I decided that wasn't going to happen. That being said, I was putting in 200+ miles a week, doing hill repeats, interval training, and general speed work, while also running at least once a week and weightlifting two to three times a week for cross-training.

You rode with a partner, Andy. Would you recommend riding with someone? What was great about having a partner? (I really enjoyed your end-of-day summaries, by the way.)
I'm glad you enjoyed them, Mike—they were a lot of fun to put together, that's for sure. I ALWAYS recommend riding with someone. I think from a safety standpoint, riding with someone just makes sense. But I also think doing something that memorable is best as a shared experience. It's something Andy and I look back on with a lot of fondness and any time we reconnect (we live thousands of miles apart) it inevitably comes up in conversation.

Overall, on average, how much time do you think you spent hike-a-biking, rather than riding? Was that a disappointment?
Ha ha! That's a great question. I'd say we were a bit disappointed with how much hike-a-bike there was on the trail. I think people don't realize that the CT is a hiking trail that allows bikes, and many of the trails simply aren't suitable for MTB. Of course, the Kurt Refsniders of the world can probably hammer out some of those crazy techy trails, but for the intermediate-early advanced rider, there will be hiking ... a *lot* of hiking. I'm not sure how much of our time was spent hiking, but I would venture that it was over 10 hours.

Favorite segment? Why?
Hmmm ... I could see the San Juans being amazing if it wasn't perma-

rain the whole time, but since it was for us, definitely not that. Probably the section from Silverton to Durango, honestly.

Least favorite segment? Why?
Whichever segment includes Sargent's Mesa.

Was there ever a moment when you thought, "I'm done, this sucks?" How'd you get past it?
The first half of our ride was beautiful and sunny, with only a few downpours, so we definitely had some highs mixed in there as well. It was crazy how much of a contrast it was, though. Luckily, Andy and I are pretty much eternal optimists, and most all of the trip was a "high," minus that night and morning I mentioned above where Andy was really struggling. But again, that's where having a riding partner can be so powerful. I was able to make some hot food for us that evening, and it's amazing how hot food can raise one's spirits, and we were able to joke and laugh about the day despite its challenges. You probably don't remember, but that was the day where Andy decided to look over our food situation and we realized I was grossly unprepared for the final day of riding before Silverton. But yeah, for me, I never had a "this sucks" moment. I tried to constantly remind myself how lucky I was to be there, and how lucky I was to be doing it with such a great friend.

Was there ever a moment when you felt pure bliss and were totally happy that you were out there? (Please describe.)
Definitely. In general, any day we climbed above tree line was an amazing experience for me. As an Oregonian, we don't have a lot of peaks above 11,000 feet (only one, actually), so getting to hang out around 10,000 and 11,000 feet and ride these pristine singletrack lines through hilly meadows was incredibly inspiring. But I also remember Buena Vista being a truly blissful moment. There was a huge storm cloud chasing us the last 20 miles into town, but we had a tailwind and it's a nice gravel road all the way in, so we hauled ass and got to our motel just before the storm hit. We got all cleaned up and then went out for beers and food at a Eddyline Brewery, and I just remember thinking, *It doesn't get any better than this.* We also had a moment early on at a grocery store where we both were low on food when we rolled into town and impulse bought the crap out of that grocery store. We then proceeded to tuck-in and inhale food for about 20 minutes straight. I remember looking back at the time lapse Andy did of our pile of food and laughing out loud reflecting on how purpose-driven we were as we devoured every item of food in sight.

Your videos are amazing. How much planning and work went into making those?
We didn't have a plan going into it, and Andy was the true mastermind behind the camera. He shot all the footage, including all of the drone shots. But as he and I discussed what we would try to film as we rode along the trail, I suggested that he shoot beautiful shots throughout the day and then we sit down and discuss the ride each night, using the footage of the day as sort of a highlight reel. At least that was what I wanted to do. Andy took a bit of a different angle with his video, which was incredible to watch as a separate perspective.

Any bits of advice for someone thinking about riding the Colorado Trail?
Hmmm ... I guess I'd say it's more accessible than people think, but that no one should go into such an endeavor lightly. It would not make a good first bikepacking experience, that's for sure. I think it's important to get some solid weekender trips in and maybe even a longer one as well (four to six days) so that you can dial in your setup—that is really crucial out on the trail and you don't want to have bags or gear that you're fiddling with throughout the experience—it's hard enough of an endeavor without having to worry about your bags falling off or your gear breaking. Don't do that to yourself! And TEST YOUR RIDING GEAR AS WELL. I could go on for a long time, now that I think about it, so I'll stop there.

Note: Ben is still riding a bunch, and you can follow his escapades on his blog: pedalspacksandpinots.com. For their videos, search Ben's name on YouTube and you'll get a ton of CT-related material. The full story-vid can also be found by looking for "2017 Bikepacking the Colorado Trail."

ANDY BRUBAKER INTERVIEW

What made you want to try this endeavor?
I did a lot of cycling and backpacking in my young adult life. I was really interested in the concept of long trails, whether hiking or biking—the AT, PCT, GDMBR, CT, etc. I enjoyed the experience of shorter two-to-four day trips and wanted to explore what extending a trip would be like. Mountain biking is my favorite method of outdoor recreation, and I love Colorado, so it was a natural fit.

Overall, did you enjoy riding the CT?
Short Answer: Yes.
Long Answer: I have a three-year old child right now, and the overall experience of the two is rather similar. Some moments are blissful, some moments are REALLY hard, and there's a lot of monotony. In the big picture, I'm absolutely glad that I did it. I don't think I'd do it again (although bikepacking smaller sections sounds great), but I'm absolutely glad I accomplished it. I was pretty sure I was going to quit about three days before the end, but managed to gut it out and finish. Definitely a good choice. Things that are important aren't always fun in the moment, but they're definitely worth doing.

When you look back at your experience, what comes to mind?
I am immensely glad I had a partner like Ben. He pushed me when I needed it, I was able to encourage him when he needed it, and having someone to laugh and suffer with during the endeavor made it that much more meaningful. Choose your adventure partners well! The generosity of trail angels, trail adopters, and other CT travelers we met along the way was also incredible. So, despite some of the most scenic views I've ever seen, the people are what spring to mind first. But the views were incredible, too.

Would you do it again?
Probably not, but I'm still glad I did it! I'd do section rides or considering hiking it for a different experience, though.

Did you train a lot? What was your training regimen?
I rode my bike trainer a lot to prepare and followed a century training plan. I also did a mountain bike race and one or two bikepacking trips before to prepare. If I'd have had the time (and

completely avoided injury, which I did not), I would have done more gravel or mountain bike long rides to get more saddle time in, but that's tricky when working full time and when you live in northern Indiana. So, the trainer was my friend (frenemy?).

You rode with a partner, Ben Handrich. Would you recommend riding with someone? What was great about having a partner?
I absolutely recommend riding with a partner. I mentioned before how helpful Ben was. The emotional support was huge, as was the help with crucial decision making: Should we push to get off the ridge and beat the storm, or hunker down under this tree for who knows how long? Do we have enough food to make it to the next resupply, or do we need to detour off-route to get more? Is this a safe place to camp? Being mentally and physically fried and having a friend to help make decisions and be an emergency support person was invaluable. Plus, Ben's a great friend and it was awesome to spend so much time together.

Overall, on average, how much time do you think you spent hike-a-biking, rather than riding? Was that a disappointment?
I wish I had actual data for this. Some days we rode more than we walked, but a lot of days, especially toward the end, we hiked more than we rode. It's a hiking trail that allows mountain bikes, so long chunks of it are utterly unrideable. Those tend to be the most beautiful sections, though, so I guess you get more time to enjoy them that way. Although pushing a 50-pound bike up a hill tends not to be very enjoyable.

Favorite segment? Why?
Most beautiful section was segments 22 and 23 right before descending into Silverton. Almost the entire thing is above treeline, so the views are incredible. But this was also the day we hiked the most, so not my favorite riding section. I also really enjoyed the section from Kenosha Pass to Breckenridge. Lots of fun, rideable trail.

Least favorite segment? Why?
Sargents Mesa. This was probably the flattest section of unrideable trail I've ever seen. Picture the rocky bottom of a stream, remove the stream, and that's what you've got. I know this section is polarizing and some people love it, but that's not me. Some people also claim they love eating ghost peppers, and I'm not jumping on that train any time soon.

Was there ever a moment when you thought, "I'm done, this sucks?" How'd you get past it?
The night before segments 22 and 23. I was exhausted, very hungry, I couldn't get warm, and I wasn't having fun anymore. I made a plan—get through the night, bail to Lake City in the morning, get a hotel until my wife could come get me. Giving myself permission to quit gave me some peace. But I woke up the next morning, felt better, and decided to give it a shot. Getting through that moment was what I'm most proud of about the entire experience.

Was there ever a moment when you felt pure bliss and were totally happy that you were out there? (Please describe.)
Descending into Durango, I was ecstatic. I was incredibly proud of myself for completing the trail, the riding was fun and manageable, the sun was shining, there was a burrito with my name on it somewhere in Durango, and I couldn't stop smiling.

Your videos are amazing. How much planning and work went into making those?
I had some general ideas of the types of shots I wanted to do, but I really didn't know how I wanted to tell the story until I was done. Once I went over all the footage a storyboard eventually formed in my head, but it took a while for the story to reveal itself. There was so much to tell. Admittedly, I ended up showcasing more of the highs than the lows, but several hours of a cursing, dirty, tired cyclist pushing his bike doesn't make the most enjoyable viewing. The hardest part of the filming was making us stop, get out the drone, fly it around and try to get some good footage, pack it all up, ride some more, and then do the same thing 20 minutes later. It added time to the trip, and the camera gear added several pounds of weight we did NOT want to carry, but having the video was definitely worth the extra effort.

Any bits of advice for someone thinking about riding the Colorado Trail?
Know that it's going to be hard, practice by doing shorter trips first, adjust to elevation as much as you can, and ride your bike a lot. Make sure you're also comfortable packing your bike, planning food for multiple days in the backcountry, and making smart decisions in sticky situations. I also strongly recommend riding with someone else for all the reasons I mentioned above. Be prepared for an incredible experience!

INTERVIEW WITH BILL MANNING OF THE COLORADO TRAIL FOUNDATION

Bill Manning recently retired as Executive Director of The Colorado Trail Foundation. Not surprisingly, he's a no-nonsense, down-to-earth kind of guy. He was kind enough to chat with me about his experiences on The Colorado Trail, share some wisdom for bikepackers, and talk about the philosophy of the CT Foundation and what they're working on.

How are things going at the CT Foundation?
We are thriving and feeling fortunate. The year 2020, with Covid and all, was an unusual year, as it was for everyone, but we came out of it in good shape. We lost some momentum, though, and had to cancel most of the trail crew work and celebrations for volunteers and supporters.

Overall, our supporters came through with many contributions, and financially we did better than break even.

In terms of trail use, numbers went up in 2020—largely due to Covid and how cooped up everybody felt. Numbers were up 50% from the previous year. Completion certificate requests traditionally total about 400 in given year; in 2020 about 600 people requested completion certificates.

My only worry is that The Colorado Trail is so wonderful, and people get deep enjoyment, but the enjoyment might be diminished somewhat because more people are using the trail. There are many out-of-staters seeking an experience in Colorado, and that adds to the stewardship work. Plus, we have to be mindful of Colorado's population growth, which inevitably leads to more folks out on the CT.

In your estimation, how many folks bikepack the CT every summer?
About 200 in a typical year. Out of that, about 100 do the Colorado Trail Race, which is unsupported and kind of do-it-on-your-own.

In your estimation, how long does it take a typical bikepacker to finish the entire thing?
I'd say about 16 days for an enjoyable trip. Basically, anywhere from 15

to 18 days is typical for a recreational bikepacker. Lots of times, folks hear about the racers completing in a week or less, so they think they could do it faster. Even a 10-day trip, in my view, is race pace. You might be able to go fast like that, but I don't think you'd enjoy it as much. You really miss out on soaking in the scenery and solitude.

Do you have any advice or wisdom for aspiring bikepackers?
Oh, big time. Cyclists should choose shoes that are easy to hike in. It'll make a huge difference to have grippy soles and shoes that you can walk in comfortably because of the number of miles you'll be pushing your bike. I think whether you choose clipless or flat pedals is a personal choice.

I've read in a few places that The Colorado Trail is about 90% rideable, which wasn't exactly my experience. In terms of mileage, how much hike-a-bike should a bikepacker be prepared to endure?
The data I've seen suggests that it's pretty common to hike-a-bike 80 to 100 miles on a typical CT trip. Racer types might not have to hike quite that far. Older cyclists might be pushing their bike more miles than that. So out of the 540 total miles, roughly, that's 18 to 20% of the total mileage.

Cyclists I've talked to have pointed out that if you were to calculate that on a total hours basis, it would be much closer to 50/50—which means half your time on the trail will be spent hiking with your bike.

What's your favorite Segment? How come?
Segment 23, Carson Saddle to Stony Pass. The views are just so grand, and it's also very physically challenging, it's a roller coaster of 400 to 500-foot climbs, and man you really feel it at 12,000 feet.

Do you have a least favorite Segment?
I don't have one; I think it's all good. I really enjoy the diversity of the experience of spending time at 5,000 feet and then going through the many altitudes with different vegetation, and then you get to alpine tundra. All that variety really adds to it. Plus, it's not all about the wilderness. I think lots of CT hikers and bikers really love these Colorado mountain towns, and spending time there.

How much training do you think a biker should do to get ready?
That would be another one of my recommendations, and it's a hot-button topic for me. We've got some really incredible athletes who can get off the couch and go do something like the CT with a very good success rate, and sometimes they recommend this to everyone. But couch-to-

adventure folks are really upper-echelon and there are not many people like that. If you're not elite like that, you can injure yourself. You really need to train. Training can help reduce the chance of injury. Preparing for the journey also makes the experience more enjoyable.

For bikers, don't forget about weight training for the legs. Do lots of stairs to help train. Find a stadium or a tall building and do repetitions.

What makes The Colorado Trail so special? Do you think there's something magical about experiencing the entire thing?
For cyclists, it's one of the few long trails that's open to bicycling, so that's on the unusual side. It's just about 500 miles, so not too long, but it's not doable in one day, either. It's a really great adventure. Crossing over and ending up on the opposite side of the Rockies is just a special experience. You get up to a high point almost every day where you can look back and see almost 100 miles and think, wow, that's where I was. Plus, the people you meet along the way are real good folks. They are enjoying the CT as much as you are, which is pretty special as well.

What's your personal experience with the trail? (Hiked, biked, how many times, etc.)
I've done the whole thing through just once, and have cobbled sections together in a variety of forms: bike, hike, horse, and unicycle.

Speaking of that, there was a guy unicycled the whole thing. He had a saddle stuffer and a small pack, stopped in towns pretty frequently, and he made it the whole way. But he broke the rules by riding though the wilderness areas. The Foundation did not champion his accomplishment because of that.

The CT for a bicyclist involves the detours. They are pretty nice routes, very scenic, kind of a break from the singletrack. At the Foundation, we ask that cyclists pay attention to the regulations. The detours are in all of our publications, so we make it easy for cyclists to follow the correct route, and we sure appreciate those that do.

Do you ever get complaints about cyclists on the Trail?
The main incidents that frustrate folks are when cyclists are going too fast for their sight distance and scare someone. Or worse, they might run into a hiker or spook a horse and get their rider bucked off. I like to boil it down to courtesy, and that's really all it takes. Choose your speed in regard to terrain, but also according to sight distance.

What are some of the things you're working on to make the CT a better experience?

Since inception we've wanted to get The Colorado Trail off the roads, and are still working hard on that. Road sections on the hiking route have shrunk to about 100 miles, and we're still chipping away by rerouting the trail. But we can't make those decisions on our own—there's the Forest Service, private landowners, environmental analysis, archeological issues, plant and wildlife concerns.

We're also constantly working to preserve the entire Trail, which is mostly about managing runoff. That takes water diversions, which are laborious to build, and we need them about every 100 feet. It's a big job, we like doing it, we have great volunteers, and have a great volunteer adoption program. Adopters "own" a certain section of the trail—keeping it clear, repairing diversions, just maintaining it. And we have trail crews for big projects. All this is managed by the Foundation. People contribute as volunteers to keep these things going.

Still, there are a few places that really suck. Beyond Marshall Pass there's some old trail route that goes straight up and straight down every hillside. Over the years, the water has carried away every bit of soil. On the other hand, there's a segment or two that reminds you how good we've got it elsewhere. The biggest reason for trail erosion is simple: You can't align a trail on the fall line. It will end up being a gully full of rocks every time. We inherited that trail in this shape, and really need to reroute it.

How can the mountain biker community help keep The Colorado Trail a sacred place?
Contribute, either by donating or volunteering. We sure could use a few more trail crew participants every year. We'd like to fill out the rest of the crew slots—currently we're at about 90%. We have a few cycling folks who've adopted a section. You can use your bike to adopt [and do the work needed], but it's not advisable. You're stopping so frequently, and it's easier to carry equipment on foot. There's an adopter waitlist currently; you can always sign up for that. A few open every year. There are 84 adoptable sections in total.

Any question you'd like to answer that I haven't asked?
Maybe not all cyclists know this, when they hit the trail for a ride, somebody built that. Somebody takes care of it. I don't think all cyclists know the amount of work that went into building that trail. It would be great if folks paid it back by helping fix or maintain the trail.

SURVEY OF COLORADO TRAIL BIKEPACKERS

While writing this book, I posted a link on various social media sites—mostly Facebook communities centered around the CT—and collected responses from bikepackers over the course of several months. Some of it is quite interesting, and lots of it helped confirm some theories I'd held. Like how lousy Sargents Mesa is, and how long it takes most folks to finish. I've collected some of the more typical and noteworthy responses below.

WHAT MADE YOU DECIDE TO TRY THIS BOLD ENDEAVOR?

- I turned 50.
- Looked fun while I was hiking the CT—saw many bikes, and wanted to try it.
- New adventure.
- I like camping and biking and bikepacking and the mountains.
- Seemed like an impossible challenge ... which is totally up my alley!
- Had three weeks off, planned a hike in Europe and it got canceled, so I was trying to find an alternative.

DID YOU COMPLETE THE RIDE?

- Yes = 55%
- No = 18%
- Not yet, but plan to = 27%

DID YOU RIDE ALONE, OR WITH A GROUP?

- All by my lonesome = 55%
- With a partner = 18%
- With a bunch of other fools = 27%

HOW OLD WERE YOU WHEN YOU COMPLETED?

- 20 to 29 = 25%
- 30 to 39 = 20%
- 40 to 49 = 22%
- 50 + = 33%

ARE YOU MALE, FEMALE, NON-BINARY?

- Boy = 72%
- Girl = 28%

IF YOU MADE IT ALL THE WAY, HOW MANY DAYS DID IT TAKE?

- 7 = 29%
- 8 = 14%
- 16 = 29%
- 17+ = 43%

DID YOU RIDE THE ENTIRE THING, INCLUDING THE DETOURS, OR DID YOU SKIP SOME STUFF? IF YOU DID SKIP, WHAT DID YOU MISS OUT ON?

There was no numerical data, but a variety of answers coalesced around two schools of thought: some skipped the detours; others were adamant about riding "every square inch."

DID YOU COMPLETE ALL AT ONCE, OR OVER THE COURSE OF A FEW SUMMERS?

- All at once = 56%
- In stages = 11%
- Didn't finish—yet = 33%
- Didn't finish and don't plan to = 0%

DID YOU HAVE ANY MECHANICAL ISSUES? IF YES, WHAT HAPPENED? HOW'D YOU SOLVE THE PROBLEM?

- This, too, provided a wealth of responses. Here are some highlights:
- One of our party this year blew out a pedal on Seg 17. He had to take county roads and highway to our destination pushing on the stem.
- Front fork losing all air. Repaired in Salida.
- Yes. Broken pedal. Had to ride to a town and try another day.
- One flat tire, fixed with a $1 bill and new tube.
- None.
- I've done it 3 times now. In 2015, my light system broke (the connector between my dynamo-hub and the light) and could not be repaired. Additionally, my shifter exploded and I was left with a single speed. In 2019, I crashed and broke a spoke, bent the wheel and bent the handlebar. Zero issues in 2020.
- Lots of flat tires. Seven between the two of us. Go tubeless.
- Screws that hold my seat bag stripped. I ziptied the bag's frame to my seatpost.
- Brakes not strong enough.
- Rear hub exploded, had to buy a new wheel in Salida.

DID YOU BRING A STOVE AND/OR A TENT?

- Full tent + stove = 45%
- Full tent + no stove = 9%
- Tarp + stove= 0%

- Tarp + no stove = 27%
- I sleep in a hammock, like a sailor, don't care about stove/no stove = 0%
- So far all of our rides have ended in townhomes, motels, camping trailers, or supported camps = 9%
- We did it in stages and would ride from camp = 9%

WHAT KIND OF A BIKE DID YOU HIKE WITH—I MEAN, RIDE?

- Full suspension 29er = 54%
- Full suspension 26 or 27.5 = 0%
- Hardtail 29er = 37%
- Hardtail 26 or 27.5 = 0%
- Fat bike = 9%
- Singlespeed = 0%
- Unicycle = 0%

HOW MUCH DID YOU TRAIN BEFOREHAND? (FEEL FREE TO GIVE DETAILS ON NUMBER OF MONTHS OF TRAINING, TOTAL MILEAGE, LONGEST RIDE, TYPE OF RIDING.)

- About eight months of craziness. But it wasn't enough. Longest ride was 55 miles, but did 300 miles in five days in June to sort of prep.
- Spent a year training. All on a spreadsheet, too detailed to list here. Lots of miles, both biking and hiking.
- Lots of training—in Florida.
- Lots?
- Depends on the year. I don't really train. I just ride and enjoy. Last year, I did ride a 24-hour hill climb (Everesting), several 100+ mile rides including a 200-mile ride and a 300-mile ride. I mostly just ride when I'm feeling like it and when inspiration hits.
- Lots.
- I'm always in training.
- Outside of general fitness, four training rides in Mid-Atlantic with one 60-miler thrown in to practice with gear.
- Five months. Still not enough.

OVERALL, DO YOU FEEL YOU PLANNED WELL?

- Yes = 63%
- No = 19%
- Maybe = 18%

WHAT DO YOU WISH YOU'D KNOWN BEFORE STARTING OUT?

- How hard it is to walk miles and miles in bike shoes.
- How difficult the southern sections are compared to north where we did our training and planning.
- That the beginning is so goddamn hard!
- Biking way harder than hiking.
- Would've travelled a bit lighter.
- How much time is spent hike-a-biking. I read about it, but experiencing it is different.
- I always run out of food and that is hard. But my frame is XS and it is hard to carry much in such a small frame.
- I wish someone had told me that Princeton Hot Springs had a bar with 24-hour menu and they will make you a burger.
- Bring spare pedals.
- How painful Segments 16 and 17 were going to be.
- Either spend more on a decent bike (I picked mine up off Craigslist) or know that after one week, altitude would catch up to me. Struggled above 12k.
- Take the tip someone recommended of not buying return flight until you're near completion (having a set date stressed me out a little).
- Take a tent, better rain pants, and better cold weather gloves.

WHAT WAS YOUR FAVORITE THING ABOUT RIDING THE COLORADO TRAIL?

- The beauty and the solitude.
- Spending so much quality time with my son, who was 15. I think he's the youngest thru-biker.
- The work.
- People.
- The views and how much fun descending a fully loaded bike still is.
- The flow.
- The beautiful moments in nature. Feeling connected to nature. The early sunrise and sunsets with the alpenglow. The joy of such a simplistic existence ... pedal, eat, drink, sleep, repeat. Sleeping under a full moon.
- Views of Colorado.
- Camaraderie with friends. Scenery. Challenge.
- Just being outside and admiring beautiful scenery! Snowstorm was cool because I got to experience the region in so many different ways.
- Challenge, amazing riding, scenic.

WHAT WAS YOUR LEAST FAVORITE THING?

- Lousy trail that wasn't even very walkable.
- Bugs and all the snow we ran into because we did an early season start.
- The work.
- Heat.
- We hit some miserable weather in the San Juans.
- The hike-a-bike.
- Monsoons! Argh! Why does it have to rain so much! Terrain that is all ripped up by motorized bikes. Trash.
- Segment 17.
- The detours.
- Losing all light power on Seg 28 around 9 PM with about seven miles to go, plus mileage to get into town ... just wanted to finish, but phew, that was mentally tough, and scary. Probably should have camped one more night, but I also didn't have any food left and had only eaten a pop tart plus two bars in the day. Needless to say, I was hangry.
- Front fork issues stopping me for a bit.

DID YOU EVER HAVE ANY SKETCHY MOMENTS? IN OTHER WORDS, DID YOU CRASH, GET STUCK IN A TERRIBLE STORM, RUN OUT OF FOOD OR WATER, GET SICK, OR RUN INTO A BEAR OR MOUNTAIN LION, ETC.? GIVE US THE SAD AND HARROWING DETAILS, PLEASE.

- Storm on Spring Creek Pass.
- Yes, to crashing: fell 100ft down a ravine, thought I broke my arm.
- Rained for three days straight, sucked being in a tarp.
- Got chased off two ridges by lightning, yuck.
- It was so hot, making water an issue.
- Ran out of water on bike detour. Very hot, sunburn/dehydration/exhaustion.
- We hit some really cold rain for a day straight in the San Juans. It's good there aren't any places to bail out there, because I think I would have.
- Late in the season, ran out of water and got near heat exhausted
- I've crashed, been stuck in too many storms to count, run out of food at least once every year, ran out of water once, heard a mountain lion once on Kenosha.
- We've been lucky. Worst was my buddy blowing out a pedal on Seg 17 and detouring on roads. Second, maybe doing Seg 1 and 2 in one day. Third, maybe the hot dogs we were fed by the trail angels at the end of Seg 17.
- Nothing too hairy. After a snowstorm on section 6, I wasn't lost lost,

but was off the trail (50-100 yards) and couldn't find it so I was hike-a-biking up some nasty steep inclines trying to figure out where the trail was. Got a full-body workout throwing my bike up and over fallen tree logs!

- Two minor crashes, both on switchbacks. Thunderstorms twice daily. Almost getting hit by lightning over Tenmile Range.

WHAT WAS YOUR MOST FAVORITE SEGMENT? (ONLY INCLUDING SEGMENTS THAT RECEIVED VOTES.)

- Segment 23: Carson Saddle to Stony Creek Pass = 36%
- Segment 25: Bolam Pass to Hotel Draw Road = 27%
- Segment 6: Kenosha to Gold Hill = 27%
- Segment 22: Spring Creek Pass to Carson Saddle = 18%
- Segment 27: Hotel Draw Road to Kennebec Pass = 18%
- Segment 8: Copper Mountain to Tennessee Pass = 9%
- Holy Cross/Mt. Massive Detour = 9%
- Segment 11: Mt Massive to Clear Creek Road = 9%

WHY?

- So gorgeous and mostly rideable.
- I had several that were favorites. The San Juans are amazing. We also went back and hiked all the wilderness sections we detoured around. Well worth the trip back.
- Met cool people.
- The trail rides really well, you're still fresh(ish) and I have a lot of good memories from that area.
- Flow, views.
- Cataract Lake.
- Phenomenal views and the Georgia pass downhill.
- Beautiful scenery!
- Amazing views and riding at over 13,000 feet.

WHAT WAS YOUR LEAST FAVORITE SEGMENT? (ONLY INCLUDING SEGMENTS THAT RECEIVED VOTES.)

- Segment 17: Sargents Mesa to Highway 114 = 55%
- Segment 16: Marshall Pass to Sargents Mesa = 18%
- Segment 1: Waterton Canyon to South Platte Trailhead = 18%
- Segment 2: South Platte River to Little Scraggy Trailhead = 9%
- Lost Creek Detour = 9%

WHY?

- Lousy riding.
- So many bugs and so rocky.
- Steep.
- So hot!
- Seems to never end!
- Hot, rocky uphill.
- Sargents. The longest segment ever. And it's haunted, maybe. So creepy. I swear it felt like someone was watching me the whole time.

WOULD YOU RIDE THE CT AGAIN, IF GIVEN THE OPPORTUNITY?

- Yes = 100%
- No = 0%
- Maybe = 0%

WHY/WHY NOT?

- Yes, but would need to seriously gird my loins, though.
- It's an amazing experience. Who wouldn't want to do it again?
- It's there.
- I'd bring lighter bike and train more for hills.
- It took me a few months to say yes I'd do it again.
- It's such a great way to see the state that I'd love to take some friends next time.
- I've done it three times now and plan to do it again this summer.
- Because it's awesome.
- I want to do it all at once.

WHAT ADVICE WOULD YOU GIVE SOMEONE WHO'S PLANNING ON DOING THE TRAIL?

- Train your ass off.
- Make sure you have comfortable shoes to walk and ride in.
- Southbound is way harder than northbound, plan for SO much hike-a-bike.
- Slow down and enjoy it.
- Train!
- Ride at altitude for a few days before starting.
- Just go for it!
- Get real comfortable hiking shoes.
- Enjoy every bit of it. Even the hard parts are amazing!

- Shit happens.
- Mentally prepare for issues.
- If you're not used to elevation or advanced technical riding, be prepared to go slower and embrace the suck.
- Don't make it your first bikepacking trip like I did.

LAST QUESTION: DID RIDING THE COLORADO TRAIL CHANGE YOU IN ANY PROFOUND WAY?

- It gave me deep confidence to handle anything I might want to take on. I'm also still mesmerized by the beauty. Planet Earth is a pretty amazing place.
- Special bond with my son. No way to really describe it.
- Yes, I'm more capable than I think I am.
- Not really.
- Probably toughened me up a bit.
- No.
- I don't think so. I mean, maybe. But probably not.
- I'm doing this in sections with a small group of friends. We are making memories and becoming closer friends as a result.
- Yes, realized that having my friends was one of my favorite things.
- Reminded me that I am strong and capable.
- I am now addicted to bikepacking races.

PACKING CHECKLIST

Here's a handy checklist of items you might want to carry with you. *The Colorado Trail Guidebook* also has lots of information on this subject.

RIDING CLOTHES (FROM HEAD-TO-TOE)

- helmet (duh, obvious)
- riding cap, balaclava, or buff
- sunglasses
- eyeglasses (if you need them)
- comfortable riding shirt
- armsleeves or long-sleeve shirt
- hooded rain jacket
- rain pants
- gloves (I prefer full-finger)
- bike shorts
- chamois
- socks for regular riding
- comfortable shoes for riding and hiking (flats or clip-in)

Optional

- warm socks for cold/morning rides (wool is good)
- heavy gloves (for rainy days, cold mornings—especially if your hands get cold easily)

CAMP AND SLEEPING OUTFIT

- warm beanie or cap (could be same as riding cap)
- sleeping shirt
- pajama bottoms, sweats or long-johns
- sleep socks
- warm camp jacket (optional if you decide that your warm riding clothes and rain jacket will suffice)
- camp shoes/sandals (also sort of optional,
- but I recommend them)

LODGING AND BEDDING

Must-Have:
- tent (or bivy) with rain cover (it will rain, I promise)
- sleeping pad
- sleeping pad repair kit
- inflatable pillow (or stuffsack that doubles as a pillow)
- warm sleeping bag
- fire-making tools (lighter, matches, fero rod)

Optional
- sleeping bag liner
- ground cover (Tyvek works fine)

KITCHEN AND PANTRY

Must-Have
- all-tool/leatherman (absolutely need one with a knife and pliers)
- water-holder system—CamelBak, water bottles, bladder
- water purification system

Optional
- cup
- pot (usually part of cook stove)
- spoon/spork/knife
- cook stove
- gas canister

BIKE GEAR

Must-Have
- multi-tool
- spare tubes
- pump
- tire levers
- extra chain
- chain-breaking tool
- chain lube and cleaning towel

Optional
- brake pads
- shoe cleat and bolts
- tubeless repair kit tube patch kit
- dropper-post lube

TECH

Must-Have
- headlamp
- cell phone
- charger and cords
- GPS system (phone or otherwise)
- CT Trail Books (including this one)
- backup battery

Optional
- GPS tracker (Garmin, et al)
- smart watch
- workout tracking app (Strava, etc)
- satellite beacon/phone
- inspiring book/reading material

PERSONAL CARE

Must-Have
- sunscreen
- toothbrush
- toothpaste
- camp towel
- soap
- nail clippers
- ibuprofen
- prescription medicine
- basic first-aid kit

Optional
- lip balm
- chamois cream
- deodorant

PACKING + STORAGE

Must-Have

- water bottle cage (in frame or somewhere else)
- handlebar bag + harness
- feed bag
- frame bag
- seat bag
- garbage bag (for junk)

Optional

- hanging bag (for food—seat bag can serve this purpose)
- cord/rope for hanging food
- trowel (for handling/burying your business)

RESOURCES

LOGISTICAL INFORMATION

COLORADO TRAIL FOUNDATION WEBSITE

This site has it all—including a way to purchase the *Guidebook* and the *Databook*. Both are great resources. Read the *Guidebook* before you go, and take the *Databook* with you, if you don't want to schlep both in your pack. coloradotrail.org

FAROUT COLORADO TRAIL APP

Download it to your phone from the app store. Make sure you get the CT bike route maps. This is an absolute necessity, and has tons on information in addition to clarity on directions, vertical data, water sources, camping spots, and detours. They've also just added a check-in feature, so loved ones can follow your journey. Works on GPS, so there are no worries about data or cell connection, and you can run your phone in airplane mode, saving precious battery power.

MTBPROJECT.COM

Peruse and read up on the CT from a rider's perspective. Has listings, details, and photos on all segments. Also, the MTB Project's phone app is a good complement to FarOut. Both track exactly where you are, and even what direction you're facing. A great preventative for going the wrong way.

WEBSITES AND BLOGS

bikepacking.com
ridingwild.org
www.singletracks.com/bike-trails/colorado-trail
oneofsevenproject.com/colorado-trail-guide-bikepacking
www.johnnestler.com
pedalspacksandpinots.com

VIDEOS

Ben Handrich and Andy Brubaker's entire CT trip, "Highs and Lows on the Colorado Trail - A Bikepacking Story

Ryan Van Duzer's Colorado Trail series

ACKNOWLEDGMENTS

With any physical endeavor, there are a whole host of folks who deserve deep appreciation and credit for their help and guidance. And with any writing endeavor, too, there's often a very patient cohort who've provided inspiration, feedback, deadlines, and encouragement—so much so that the book itself never would have come about if it weren't for them. This is one such book.

I'd like to thank my wife Andrea Dupree for tolerating my long absences over the course of three summers. I'm eternally indebted to her patience at my bike-related spending, for the many hours I spend in the garage messing around with my bike and gear, for dropping me off that early August morning at Waterton Canyon, and for watching our kids when I was in the wild. Many thanks, too, for her feedback and help with the manuscript, especially for calling attention to my overuse of words like "beautiful," "lovely," and "lousy." And thanks to my daughters Emmy and Jo, for not only being fun, brilliant kids, but for humoring their dad when he endlessly blabs about his adventures. You are all an inspiration, and I am one very lucky guy.

I am also deeply grateful for the support I received from the Bonfils-Stanton Foundation's Livingston Fellowship program, in particular Gary Steuer and Jesse King, for going along with the idea that riding the Colorado Trail would be a worthwhile leadership learning experience. Without their good will, I wouldn't have seriously thought of doing this.

Thanks also goes out to Dr. Ian Dickey, the orthopedic surgeon who removed a mass of precancerous scar tissue in my left calf back in 2017. I'm also eternally grateful to my all-time riding partner Ed Itell, who first took me mountain biking in 2001. We rode simple 26-inch rim-brake hardtails, and he basically taught me how to ride, and vividly showed that, if you believe it, you can pretty much ride up, down, and over just about anything. I will, however, never forgive him for leading me down Poison Spider/Portal Trail in Moab that one time. Thanks also to Michael Elijah Wenham, who drove me out to Buena Vista, fed and entertained me the night before I embarked on the second leg of my CT journey. Likewise, thanks to the good folks at Absolute Bikes who supplied me with a new rear wheel when my old hub shattered, and for the kind folks in various towns who provided me rooms to rest in, food to scarf down, and supplies to keep me going. Much appreciation also to the wonderful baristas at St. Mark's Coffee House on 17th Avenue in Denver, for all those finely crafted lattes that fueled the writing of this book.

A thousand miles worth of gratitude also goes to Caleb Seeling and Derek Lawrence at Bower House, for not only being interested in the book, but for their guidance and support. Deep appreciation, too, for Scott Gurst, head coach at Brute Squad, for his insights and training wisdom.

My endless and deep appreciation also goes out to all the good people I met on the trail, all the good vibes they provided, along with food, directions, and energy, specifically trail angels Pooh and Jan, and the Jeep guy who drove me up and over Stony Pass and into Silverton when I'd lost all hope. And to JC, my shadow from Segment 2 all the way to Leadville; I wish we'd exchanged contact info. I hope you are well and remember our time together as fondly as I do.

A million thanks go out to all the volunteers who work on the Colorado Trail, and to Bill Manning, Gudy Gaskill, and Jerry Brown. You've made something very impressive, indeed. We are all forever grateful.

Finally, I want to express my love and appreciation for my father, a career mailman, who traveled more miles on foot than I ever will on two wheels, a man who taught me to work hard and believe in the inherent goodness of the world. I am so very lucky to be your son.

And finally, this book is dedicated to the memory of my mother, who showed me what real bravery looks like.

ABOUT THE AUTHOR

Michael J. Henry is co-founder and Executive Director of Lighthouse Writers Workshop, the largest independent literary arts center in the Rocky Mountain west. He is the author of three books of poetry and has received artist fellowships from the Colorado Council on the Arts, PlatteForum, and a Livingston Fellowship from the Bonfils-Stanton Foundation. As a distance runner at the University of Rochester, he was the inaugural University Athletic Association steeplechase champion and an NCAA Division III Team All-American in cross country.

PRAISE FOR *MOUNTAIN BIKING THE COLORADO TRAIL*

"Plenty of guidebooks load you up with information. But what Michael Henry does in this invaluable pocket companion is give you real-life experience. The logistical information here tells you everything you need to know to tackle the Colorado Trail by bike in a way that is easy to digest and will prove helpful when you are out in the wild on your own. But what is even more important is this guidebook was written by someone who wants to share the dream and help you make it happen. Henry has paid his dues out on the dirt. Even more so, he taps into the real motivation of taking on such a big objective. His book also gets to the heart of why you would want to bikepack the Colorado Trail and how accomplishing the feat can help you navigate your own life."

—Doug Schnitzspahn,
Editor in Chief, *Elevation Outdoors* magazine

"Riding the Colorado Trail humbled me like no other event in my life. My first experience riding the CT wasn't one I was at peace with. I was inexperienced, arrogant and under-researched. I stumbled through many not only uncomfortable but downright dangerous situations, cursing rather than appreciating the beautiful magnitude of this beast. My ego ultimately dragged me to a finish I had no reason to celebrate. After reflecting on the trail itself and my embarrassing execution I knew I had to tackle it again. Less ego, more appreciation, more experience. The second ride many years later took me into day-long states of zen, the discomfort just a necessary offering to unlock the Trail's secrets. I pushed my body, expanded my mind, and finally appreciated that the beauty of this trail lies in the relentless challenges it throws at you around every corner. If you want an athletic challenge, do an Ironman. If you want a life experience, consider the Colorado Trail. Michael, through his own attempts, has managed to translate what has been for me impossible to articulate: what it is to take on the Colorado Trail by bike."

—Lachlan Morton,
professional biker and record holder of the CT's fastest completion time